I HURT

A Life-Changing Experience

You Can Be More Christ-like—Better Understand Yourself and Others

By Gary Morais

Resources by Gary Morais
The Professional's Tool—How to Better Understand Yourself and Others
Targeted Performance Coaching
The Executive's Tool for Strategic Performance Building
People, Performance & Profit
The Executive's Tool for Strategic Performance Building
A Management Leadership & Performance Enhancement Program

Be Transformed by the Renewing of Your Mind Copyright © 2016 by Gary Morais (Based on original work *How to Better Understand Yourself and Others* Copyright © 1989 by Gary Morais)

Scripture quotations marked (NKJV) - Scripture taken from the New King James Version®. Copyright © 1982 by Thomas Nelson. Used by permission. All rights reserved.

Scripture quotations marked (NIV) – Scripture taken from the Holy Bible, New International Version®, NIV®, Copyright © 1973, 1978, 1984, 2011 by Biblica, Inc. ™ Used by permission of Zondervan. All rights reserved worldwide. "http://www.zondervan.com" The "NIV" and "New International Version" are trademarks registered in the United States Patent and Trademark Office by Biblica, Inc.™

All rights reserved. No part of this publication may be reproduced, stored in a retrieval system, or transmitted in any form or by any means—electronic, mechanical, photocopy, recording, or any other—except for brief quotations in printed reviews, without the prior permission of the author, Gary Morais, or the Publisher.

Cover Image by Depositphotos. Used with permission.

www.kendallhunt.com
Send all inquiries to:
4050 Westmark Drive
Dubuque, IA 52004-1840

Copyright © 2021 by Gary Morais

ISBN 978-1-7924-6409-6

Kendall Hunt Publishing Company has the exclusive rights to reproduce this work,
to prepare derivative works from this work, to publicly distribute this work,
to publicly perform this work and to publicly display this work.

All rights reserved. No part of this publication may be reproduced,
stored in a retrieval system, or transmitted, in any form or by any
means, electronic, mechanical, photocopying, recording, or otherwise,
without the prior written permission of the copyright owner.

Published in the United States of America

Special Thanks

I would like to recognize several people who have contributed over the year to help make this book possible. Each of these individuals gave their precious time to move this book forward so it can have an impact on people's lives. I am forever grateful to you all.

Robert Wageneck and Gary Smyth for their kind assistance in the Scripture selections feedback and editing review.

Tom Doty for his detailed mind, input, and design for the Equipping Profile; Kim Levings for her years of helping with prayers and training design; Annie Vance, PhD, for her contribution of editing suggestions; Pastor Dr. Paul Cruz for his encouragement and prologue contributions to the first chapter; and Kathy Kelly from Kelly Productions for the book cover design and copy layout. Also, very special thanks to Susan Sorian for her Spirit-filled, gracious editorial suggestions and professional revisions that were given by God to her to make this book possible.

Also, thank you to Pastor David Guzik from Enduring Word, Pastor Tommy Schneider, and Pastor Bret Shellabarger for their pastoral directional input and Scriptural guidance, which was foundational to the purpose and content of this book.

A very special blessing and thanks to all who provided their help, guidance, prayers, and positive encouragement that inspired me to move forward in writing this book.

And, above all, to our Lord and Savior, Jesus Christ, because without His saving grace, this book would not even have been written.

Dedication

To the Lord and for His loving and saving grace and to all of God's people, that they may grow as we all journey toward becoming more Christ-like.

Table of Contents

INTRODUCTION vii
    Who Am I?—Prologue viii
    Mission Statement xvi

CHAPTER 1 FOUNDATIONAL THINKING 1

CHAPTER 2 DECISIVE THINKING
    Are You Frustrated by Your Inability to Take Charge and
    Make Decisions? 15

CHAPTER 3 SELF-ASSURED THINKING
    Learning to Trust Yourself / Increasing Your Confidence 29

CHAPTER 4 EXPRESSIVE THINKING
    Have You Been Frustrated by the Lack of Expressive
    Communication? 43

CHAPTER 5 COMPASSIONATE THINKING
    Do You Find It Easy to Pick Up on Others' Feelings? 63

CHAPTER 6 ORGANIZED THINKING
    Do You Think in a Systematic Manner? 77

CHAPTER 7 SELF-DOUBTING THINKING
    Have You Ever Been Frustrated by a Lack of Assertiveness? 93

CHAPTER 8 OVER EXPECTANT THINKING
    Have You Ever Thought of Yourself as Being Controlling? 111

CHAPTER 9 CONTRARY THINKING
    Do You Ever Feel Like People Are Telling You What to Do? 133

CHAPTER 10 SELF-DEFEATING THINKING
    Are You Hard on Yourself and Don't Accept Compliments? 151

CHAPTER 11 HYPERSENSITIVE THINKING
  Have You Ever Felt Overly Self-Conscious? 169

CHAPTER 12 SPIRITUAL SURVIVAL
  Answers to a Life-Changing Subject? 185

CONCLUSION
  Your New Beginning 191

ABOUT THE AUTHOR.. 195

Introduction

You may have picked up this book because of its title, **I Hurt**.

I Hurt is packed with solutions and practical tools for worldly issues that we all face. This book provides you with invaluable insights from a Christian counseling practice that has helped thousands of people overcome their fears, anxieties, and stresses in life. These proven solutions are based on God's truth as spoken in Romans 12:2, "... be transformed by the renewing of your mind. ..." It translates Biblical Scripture into real life, easy-to-use applications that will help you become more Christ-like and have a more fulfilling, joy-filled, and peaceful life.

Scripture calls us to be more "Christ-like" and tells us over and over again that we are to not be afraid or anxious. But how do we do this? How do we become the person that is made in God's image, to be free from our hurts, fears and anxieties?

This book is written because of a driving need to help God's People, by equipping them to reach their fullness in how they were created and to discover their God-given inner gifts and hidden strengths so they can better understand how they have been built in "the image of Christ."

I say this because I came to realize, in my own life and the lives of thousands of people I have worked with over the last 35 years, that we are wonderfully made, by a Creator that loves us. I didn't always understand this because my own personal journey in life didn't start out so wonderfully. But that's life!

You might be thinking, "Common sense tells me that I can't change my life in days, right?" I would have to agree with you; one's whole life cannot be changed in mere days. However, you can make one or two very significant changes, and surely if you complete this book in days, you will know more about yourself or others than many PhDs know from their years of going through school. "That's a big bold statement!" you may say. So, I guess you will have to read the book to find out if this statement has legs! The goal for change is simple ". . . be transformed by the renewing of your mind." Romans 12:2 (NJKV)

The reason for this book is to give you 35 years of what I have learned and experienced as a therapist in private practice, a business strategist to major corporations, an inventor of a human capital performance assessment, a CEO of a human capital consulting and technology company, a Christian counselor to pastors and churches, a disciple of my Lord and Savior, and as a father, grandfather, husband, and friend.

WHO AM I?–Prologue

Someone once said, "You aren't who you think you are; you aren't who others think you are; you are who you think others think you are." The first time I read that quote, I thought, "Wow, that's pretty sharp." Almost immediately the Holy Spirit prompted the thought, "Actually that's not true. In reality, you aren't who you think you are, you aren't who others think you are, and you aren't who you think others think you are. You are who God says you are . . . made in His image."

The issue of identity is foundational to our personal lives and well-being. Every person on the planet has an innate desire to feel loved, accepted, significant, and secure. One of the ways this desire is satisfied is through an understanding of who we are at the core of our being. Without that understanding we will, without fail, search for identity in illegitimate ways. We will examine that more closely in just a bit.

WHAT IS YOUR SELF-VIEW?

Please ask yourself this question, "What is my self-view?" Simply stated, your self-view is the way you see yourself. It is the thoughts that you have about you. These thoughts can be positive or negative. If you are like most people, your thoughts are a mixture of positive and negative.

The most important question about your self-view is not necessarily whether your thoughts are positive or negative, but are they grounded in truth? You can have positive but untrue thoughts that lead to a self-view that isn't healthy; for example, the wealthy man who has been successful in business who may think he's God's gift to mankind has a positive but unhealthy self-view. He has positive thoughts, but his thoughts lead to arrogance which is unhealthy and will hurt his relationships. On the other hand, you can also have a negative self-view based on thoughts that are just as untrue.

The most important thing about your self-view is its foundation . . . is it based on truth? Your thoughts about you produce your feelings about you, which affect your behavior, which determines the course of your life. So, as you can see, your self-view is extremely vital. Being that vital, it is crucial to make sure it is based in reality.

WHERE WE GET OUR VIEW OF OURSELVES

We get our view of ourselves from a variety of influences. Our self-view is shaped by factors such as physical size and looks, personality, popularity, athletic ability, wealth, and so on. Probably the most prominent source of our self-view is what others say to us and how they treat us, especially as we grow as children and as adolescents. The impact of the words and opinions of those around us, especially our immediate family and friends, is incalculable in the formation of our self-view.

While it is true that our closest relationships make a great impression on us, life-experiences also play a big part in our self-view. The woman who has experienced a life of mostly wonderful experiences is more likely to be positively programmed." The man who has dealt with multiple traumatic situations may be more "negatively programmed." Of course, there are exceptions as in the case of a woman who is determined to overcome her traumas by the choice of her will and personal determination. In this situation, the person often trades one warped self-view for another. What looks good to the world, in that she has overcome a negative self-view, might actually be a case of trading one false view for another. We'll talk about how to avoid the dilemma of trading false views in just a moment.

HOW OUR SELF-VIEW AFFECTS US

As we stated before, our self-view affects our entire life. The list that follows shows the concentric circles of impact of our self-view:

- Your view of you—It's probably obvious at this point that your view of you affects you.

- Your view of God—Your self-view determines how you see God. Conversely, your view of God also determines how you view you.
- Your view of others—Your self-view determines how you view and relate to those around you.

How you see yourself impacts your mental, emotional, spiritual, and even physical health. If you feel that you are so damaged that God doesn't love you and can't forgive you, that mindset will corrode your mind, emotions, spirit, body, and every relationship you have. You will experience very little joy and peace in your life. Such a view will sabotage every opportunity for real meaning you will ever have. There is no aspect of your life that your view of yourself does not affect.

WHERE WE AS BELIEVERS SHOULD GET OUR SELF-VIEW

A healthy self-view is determined by what is true, and what is true is determined not by what we or others think or say, but by what God says. As believers in Jesus Christ, what God says about us is grounded in two things:

1. What Jesus did for us
2. What Jesus says about us

The work of Christ and the Word of God are the sole determiners for what is true about us. If you have not repented of your sins and come to Jesus for salvation, you need to give this serious consideration. Otherwise, you have only you to rely on for your self-view.

Through the finality of the cross and the miracle of the resurrection, you and I, as believers, were transferred and transformed. We were relocated to a new Kingdom (Colossians 1:13) and remade into new creations (2 Corinthians 5:17). Therefore, we are not and will never again be what we once were! We are who Jesus has made us to be and who He says we are! The Word of God, which is totally true and does not lie, tells us what Jesus accomplished for us and what He has accomplished in us. It also tells us what He will accomplish through us! Immersing ourselves in the truth of the Word transforms our minds and re-calibrates our lives according to truth (Romans 12:1-2). Take time each day to get into the Bible to ingest the truth of who God is and who you are in Him. Start by reading Romans 5-8 and Ephesians 1 and be amazed!

WHO WE ARE

The Bible is full of great truths concerning who we are as believers. The following is a list of things that God calls and/or says are true about the Christian. This list is not exhaustive but is a great start. Spend time looking up the Scripture references and meditating on each phase as true of you.

Remember, regardless of your past messages or feelings, what God says is true!

Our culture loves to use the phrase, "my truth." Honestly, there is no such thing as "my truth." We don't each have our own unique truth. There is just truth, and it all belongs to God. God's truth is true and everything else is false. So, if Satan, "father of lies," starts lying to you, give him a heavy dose of truth. Think, pray, and declare the following truths out loud:

I AM . . .

- A child of God (2 Corinthians 6:18; Galatians 3:26)
- In the Beloved (Ephesians 1:5-6; Colossians 3:12)
- In Him (Ephesians 1:3-14)
- Alive in Christ (I Corinthians 15:22; Ephesians 2:4-5)
- Indwelt by the Holy Spirit (1 Corinthians 3:16; 2 Timothy 1:14)
- Under His grace (Romans 6:14; Titus 2:11)
- Lavished in His love (Ephesians 1:8; 1 John 3:1-2)
- More than a conqueror in Christ (Romans 8:37; 1 Corinthians 15:57)
- A saint (Ephesians 2:19; Colossians 1:26-27)
- Forgiven (Ephesians 1:7; 1 John 2:12)
- A friend of God (John 15:15; James 2:23)

This is just a sampling of what Jesus says is true of you!

THE IMPORTANCE OF WALKING IN WHO YOU ARE

Why is it important to walk in the truth of who you are? Walking in a Biblical self-view enables you to:

- Walk in the love of God.
- Experience the fullness of God.
- Fulfill the will of God.
- Defeat the enemy of God. Silence his lies with truth over and over and over.

- Display the glory of God.
- Do the works of God.
- Share the love of God.

FILLING IN THE OLD RUTS

Years ago, I was taught this powerful analogy of how our minds work. If you ever visit a farm and ride around it in a truck or on a tractor, one of the things you will quickly notice is the ruts in the landscape. These ruts are paths of hardened mud that have developed through the years as the truck or tractor has followed the same path day after day. As the farmer makes his or her rounds, ruts form. After a while you barely need to steer the tractor! The ever-deepening ruts will guide it for you! Our thought patterns can be the same way.

Satan loves to get us thinking in certain ways. He thrives on filling our minds with ideas and thoughts that are untrue and destructive to our well-being and relationships. Of course, when he speaks to you, he does so in what sounds like your voice using first person pronouns so that you think it's you! Over the years, as we allow these thoughts space in our minds, they form ruts in our thinking. Just like the tractor or truck, we naturally gravitate toward that line of thinking.

For example, if Satan has bombarded you with thoughts of jealousy throughout your life and you have nursed those thoughts, they have formed jealous ruts in your mind. So, when you are faced with a situation that could possibly encourage jealousy on your part, your mind goes there immediately. By the way, Satan has no clue what idea might take root in your life. He just tries throwing different things out there to see what works with you.

To overcome this tactic, we have to employ a plan to fill in the ruts. You know as well as I do that our enemy, the devil, doesn't leave us alone just because we read some verses and made some declarations. We have to keep up the fight by trading up to the truth daily, inwardly, and intentionally. How do you do that?

Here are five suggestions:

1. Cooperate with the Holy Spirit—Surrender yourself fully to the Holy Spirit. Ask Him to cleanse you, fill you, and lead you into all truth.
2. Spend time in the presence of God—Just sit and soak in God's presence, praising and thanking Him for who He is, what He has done, and what He is doing.
3. Time in the Word of God—Immerse yourself in God's Word, reading, meditating, and memorizing. Saturate your mind in God's Word daily!
4. Hearing the voice of God—Listen to what God says to you personally as He applies His Word to you and be sure to write down what He says. If you don't, I promise Satan will steal it.
5. Repeat the voice of God—Memorize Scripture and recite it to yourself and even out loud as you have opportunity. Doing this will bring peace and strength as you affirm God's Word to you.

Your understanding of being a new creation in Christ's image is critical to walking in daily victory and it needs to be grounded in scriptural truth. God's view of you trumps your view of you or anyone else's. What God says about you is true whether you believe it or not, but you will only be blessed by believing it! There is no way to walk in the abundant life without believing what God says about you! Jesus said to love your neighbor as you love yourself. Implicit in that command is to love yourself. Start today!

Prologue by: Pastor Paul Crews,
Pastor/Elder, More2Life Ministries

> *"You were taught, with regard to your former way of life, to put off your old self, which is being corrupted by its deceitful desires; to be made new in the attitude of your minds; and to put on the new self, created to be like God in true righteousness and holiness."*
>
> EPHESIANS 4:22-24 (NIV)

Transformational Learning Based Upon Romans 12:2
The Cornerstone of How to Better Understand Yourself and Others

> *"'Take away the stone,' He [Jesus] said. 'But, Lord,' said Martha, the sister of the dead man, 'by this time there is a bad odor, for he has been there four days.' Then Jesus said, 'Did I not tell you that if you believed, you would see the glory of God?' So, they took away the stone."*
>
> JOHN 11:39-41A (NIV)

The principles of *I Hurt* are to equip you to have greater personal skills, while lowering anxiety and internal fears. The stones become the metaphor for those areas within ourselves that hold us down (encumbrances) from truly living the life God desires for us. We need other people and "instruments" to remove that initial stone and raise awareness regarding the blockages in our spirits. Only when the stones are removed can we respond to the voice of God that lives in our lives.

> *"... Then Jesus looked up and said, 'Father, I thank you that you have heard me. I knew that you always hear me, but I said this for the benefit of the people standing here, that they may believe that you sent me.'"*
>
> JOHN 11:41-42 (NIV)

Developing a relationship with God is the primary foundation of all the equipping tools and chapters in this book. Without this ongoing relationship, any work done by you becomes human effort, not a Christ-centered, God-driven process.

> *"When He had said this, Jesus called in a loud voice, 'Lazarus, come out!' The dead man came out, his hands and feet wrapped with strips of linen, and a cloth around his face. Jesus said to them, 'Take off the grave cloths and let him go.'"*
>
> JOHN 11:43-44 (NIV)

Once the stones in our lives are rolled away, we need more help in learning to let go of past behaviors (the "grave cloths") and to embrace the new transformed beliefs that free us from our fears. The equipping tools and chapters in this book are designed to develop positive new transformational thinking and behavior patterns which lead you to a life of freedom of your spiritual gifts and the realization of all that God desires for you in serving Him. Hopefully this book can be a bridge to opening our hearts and minds to new learning experiences which allow us to become fully responsible for our own thoughts and behavior and not stay stuck in fears. We all have areas that need improvement; this is our human nature. Most of us by nature are receptive to thoughtful and positive suggestions for our personal and spiritual growth.

This book is the result of many years of working with people from all walks of life. It is my desire that you use what fits for your life, and use it in a positive and helpful manner to enrich your life. There may be parts of this book you already know, whereas other parts are new or enlightening. One thing for sure, as you read it you will see parts of yourself and others. Hopefully this will create an enriching experience of how to better understand yourself and others as well as enrich a greater understanding of how Jesus plays as an example to all of us.

I admire you for making the decision to equip yourself with new tools to enrich your life. My wish for you is a better life, a closer relationship with God, and a sense of joyful living.

Let's Get Started!

READ CHAPTER 1—FOUNDATIONAL THINKING

Next you will learn who you are! Then you will begin to understand Primary Relationships and Spiritual Survival and how it impacts all of our lives. Then we begin to learn about Transformational Tools or what is called thinking behavior skills. These chapters provide you with equipping tools you need for positive change so you can . . . "Be transformed by the renewing of your mind. . . ." Romans 12:2

MISSION STATEMENT

We seek to provide a Biblical approach to helping God's people transform their lives so as to glorify Christ.

Biblical coaching has God at the center. He is the source of hope, and His Word is the foundation and power for real change in the human soul, whereas modern psychological theory is deficient in that it is merely based upon studies of human behavior, and its conclusions are as varied as the humans themselves. The center of the philosophy is man himself.

In recent years, there have been great strides made in the science and study of the human brain. Studies imply that negative or destructive thought patterns give birth to more negative thought patterns (worldly thinking) and the converse is also true. But this is not merely the "power of positive thinking," but the retraining and renewing of the mind, resulting in actual physical change in the operation of the brain.

Where there is true transformation by the Word of God, the negative, humanistic behaviors can be changed by the consistent, purposeful application of God's truths. Our brain in a very real sense can be re-trained, re- programmed, or re-wired as it were. It is a physical manifestation of Biblical Truth.

We are commanded in Romans 12:2 to be transformed by the renewing of our mind and in Philippians 4:8, that if there be anything worthy of praise, to think upon these things. For the weapons of our warfare are not carnal but mighty in God, for pulling down strongholds, casting down arguments, and every high thing that exalts itself against the knowledge of God, bringing every thought into captivity to the obedience of Christ. (2 Corinthians 10:4-5)

This is an educational approach to helping God's people, training them up in a transformational process that is Biblically based, equipping them to be successful in their own lives.

> *"Be transformed by the renewing of your mind. . . . "*
>
> ROMANS 12:2 (NKJV)

"I sought the Lord, and He heard me,
And delivered me from all my fears."

PSALM 34:4 (NKJV)

"The discretion of a man makes him slow to anger, And his glory is to overlook a transgression."

PROVERBS 19:11 (NKJV)

NOTES

CHAPTER 1

FOUNDATIONAL THINKING

> *In this section we will discover several things:*
> 1. Who you are
> 2. How to understand Primary Relationships and Spiritual Survival and how each impacts our lives
> 3. What Transformational Thinking and Transformational Tools are or what is called, "new thinking skills"— based on Romans 12:2

Examine some causes of why people get mad, argue, fight, and become sad and depressed.

How does Christ fit in this seemingly worldly mess we are in?

Who Are You?

I have been asking this question to thousands of people and have found that about 95 percent of the people in the United States can't answer this question. Why? Because people don't teach their children, because they are not equipped to answer the question for themselves. How can you give what you don't have yourself?

Let's start out with some common *incorrect answers* I hear.

1. I am a manager / plumber / secretary / carpenter / waiter.
2. I am a mother/father.

3. I create software / jewelry / paintings.
4. I repair cars / clean rugs / clean houses.
5. I have great ideas.
6. I am sometimes mad and angry.
7. I am a person who doesn't trust anyone.

Here Is the Truth About Who You Are!

Who you are has nothing to do with your title, what you do (job), or your ideas or behaviors! Surprised? Well, this is how the world defines us, but it has nothing to do with "Who you are."

Who you are has to do with your intrinsic value given to you by God. These are traits like: kind, caring, loving, creative, faithful, compassionate, affectionate, forgiving, and so on. These are God-given qualities you were born with, your gifts that reflect your Creator's image. This is who you really are. Now, this doesn't mean we are perfect, because we all at times have bad behavior (sin). It bothers us when we have bad behavior because bad behavior doesn't reflect who we really are, or how we were made. Every one of us has bad behavior (sins) and that is what we all struggle with. But there is good news. We have a Savior who died for our sins, so we are free to be "who we really are—built in Christ's image." We will talk more about this later.

If you know who you are, you are less vulnerable. "How does this work?" you may be asking yourself. Let's look at an example:

A friend came over to Joe's house when he was building a picnic table in his back yard. Joe's friend says, "Why would anyone build a picnic table that looks like that? That is the goofiest table I have ever seen."

A statement like that can start an argument with Joe having to defend why he is building his picnic table that way, and Joe's reaction is, "You are stupid for not liking my table, and you are no friend of mine, so you can leave right now and get out of my life." Later Joe feels bad after he gets over his anger, then he feels guilty for overreacting. Wow, a frustrating experience, but all too common, in today's world.

In the previous example, the reason Joe overreacted and got angry was he was making the picnic table an extension of himself. In his mind, Joe was the picnic table. Sanctified common sense tells us that this is a false way to think. Why? Because Joe is much more than his ideas or what he is building. But if Joe doesn't know who he is, he is vulnerable. Does Joe's story sound familiar?

Do you, or people you know, argue or get hurt because someone doesn't agree with your ideas? Do you find yourself becoming upset if your family, friends, or coworkers don't agree with your ideas or suggestions? So how do we change this? How do we become less vulnerable?

Your first step is to be equipped by knowing "who you are."

Let's start off with what could be one of the best exercises you can do in your life. That is getting to know who you are. God gives us all gifts, or what is our intrinsic value given to us by God. This is all the great stuff that is inside, our internal gifts of the spirit.

The world has taught many of us false teaching about ourselves like:

- My ideas are who I am.
- The clothes I wear make the man / woman.
- The car I drive is who I am, and gives me value.
- I have value because I have a job title, or position of authority.
- I am a bad person, because I have had bad behavior.

> *"You are the light of the world. A town built on a hill cannot be hidden. Neither do people light a lamp and put it under a bowl. Instead, they put it on its stand, and it gives light to everyone in the house. In the same way, let your light shine before others, that they may see your good deeds and glorify your Father in heaven."*
>
> MATTHEW 5:14-16 (NIV)

What causes you to get mad, argue, fight, and become sad and depressed? Whether you are getting your feelings hurt, getting mad, feeling frustrated, or being anxious, sad, or depressed, you all have one thing in common with every other person: HOW AND WHAT YOU ARE THINKING. Your thinking determines how you will experience the world.

How you think determines how your life unfolds. I had a friend, Earl Nightingale, who was known all over the world, and he used to say, "We are what we think about." I guess this has some truth to it.

So, what are a few causes of why people end up reacting instead of responding? You can get a closer look when you read this section on Foundational Thinking.

Here's How Many People Stumble

So many people don't let their internal light shine because of internal fears that hold them back, partly because *they don't know who they are or* are unable to identify their internal light, their God-given intrinsic value.

A light is only useful if it shines, not when it is hidden. We need to let our intrinsic value (who we are) shine, and let God's light (or Holy Spirit) shine through us.

We all have thousands of ideas, and the possibilities of all our ideas matching up with others are nearly impossible. If we are relying on people to accept all our ideas before we feel accepted, then our internal goodness (our internal light—which we are) is at jeopardy every time we open our mouth. This is just not good common sense to make our ideas an extension of ourselves.

You are much more than your ideas!

Jesus recognizes who we are, and He made us to have intrinsic value that is good. He is calling us to let our light shine before men, that they may see our good deeds and praise the Father in heaven.

Let's take the first step in understanding the question—Who are you? We do so by completing the exercise on the following page.

> *"The fruit of the righteous is a tree of life, and the one who is wise saves lives."*
>
> PROVERBS 11:30 (NIV)

The fruit of the Spirit is really who we are! We must ask ourselves, what is my fruit (our internal gifts) given to me by God?

Who You Are

Who you are has nothing to do with your ideas, what you do, your behaviors, a job title, a position at work, or what you drive, where you live, or the high style clothes you have on. Who you are is always internal and positive. Sure, we all have bad behavior from time to time, but it's not who we are. When you know who you are, you are less vulnerable, because it doesn't matter what others think of you, because God has made you to be the unique person in His image who has gifts (Fruits of the Spirit). Then you are free to express your ideas without having to defend or convince others in order to give yourself value.

> "And we all, who with unveiled faces contemplate the Lord's glory, are being transformed into his image with ever increasing glory, which comes from the Lord, who is the Spirit."
>
> 2 Corinthians 3:18 (NIV)

SO, WHO ARE YOU?—AN EXERCISE

Put a check √ mark in front of each word that best describes your intrinsic God-given value—Your inherent gifts God has given you (Fruits of the Spirit).

goodness	fulfilled	forgiven	peaceful	tranquil
connected	affectionate	special	loving	comfortable
serene	kind	reconciled	satisfied	bonded
united	committed	private	forgiving	devoted
respectful	attached	cherished	confident	appreciative
humility	electrified	enthusiastic	compassionate	calm
precious	open	poor in spirit	meek	righteousness
a giver	peacekeeper	repentant	wisdom seeker	helpful
festive	servant	centered	content	serene
complacent	comfortable	joyful	ecstatic	eager
inspired	glad	pleased	blissful	cheerful
sunny	high-spirited	bright	animated	sparkling
exhilarate	jovial	frisky	self-control	God-centered
jubilant	playful	earnest	patience	passionate
humble	intense	desirous	high integrity	upright
concerned	affected	fascinated	hardy	engrossed
intriguing	absorbed	excited	curious	inquisitive
loyal	interested	inquiring	approachable	involved
transformed	trusting	united	connected	warm
valued	giving	innocent	relational	creative
sincere	gracious	desired	fun loving	caring
loyal	enterprising	monogamous	spiritual	forgiving
pretty	believer	profound	pure of heart	reverent
blessed	soft	non-envious	supportive	thoughtful
wisdom seeker	disciplined	expressive	sensitive	warmhearted
sympathetic	friendly	hopeful	understanding	open minded
demonstrative	responsive	encouraged	courageous	confidant
secure	bold	brave	daring	faithful
longsuffering	fearless	God-reliant	determined	reassured
obedient	stout-hearted	organized	treasured	understanding

CHAPTER 1 FOUNDATIONAL THINKING

List any other inherent Gifts of the Spirit you have been given by God.

_____

_____

_____

From the list, pick the top 10 and memorize them.
This is who you are!

Read your list of intrinsic values (words) three times a day until you know who you are.

What a great feeling to know who you are. God made you a great and wonderful person, whose light can shine before men, free from rejection if someone doesn't accept your ideas. By knowing who you are in God's eyes, you can have a new inner strength and joy.

EXAMPLE:

If someone came up to you and said, "You're a terrible person," you can easily say, "Well, if you really know who I am then you couldn't say that. Because who I am is . . . ," then repeat the words you picked from the previous list. That's real internal strength. Remember you are built in God's image, with real intrinsic value, and your gifts are given to you by God.

Now this doesn't mean we don't need to be responsible for our negative behaviors (sin). If we have bad behavior (sin) we do have to be responsible for it and apologize, make amends, and ask for forgiveness (repentance).

By knowing our intrinsic value, we can freely express our ideas without having to worry about rejection or rejecting others' ideas when they do not match up with our ideas.

We can thank God for this!

We have the wonderful gift of God making us in His image.

> *"Let your light so shine before men, that they may see your good works and glorify your Father in heaven."*
>
> MATTHEW 5:16 (NKJV)

Read your list of intrinsic values (words) three times a day until you know who you are.

WE NEED TO TRADE UP TO THE TRUTH TO SET OURSELVES FREE

Remember our earlier example about Joe building a picnic table in his back yard. Let's say Joe also believed 3 x 5 = 14. Yes, 14. If Joe doesn't trade-up to the truth 3 x 5 = 15 we can predict he will be fired from his accounting job, right? We also can predict this false belief (3 x 5 = 14) will negatively impact Joe and others like his family as well. So how can someone like Joe change?

This book has a section on Transformational Thinking Statement tools or what we call, "thinking trade-ups." This book is about being transformed by the renewing of your mind, in order to be equipped with "new truths to set you free." Scripture is loaded with these truths. This book is an attempt to sift out the most common everyday thinking and relationship issues that people struggle with and deliver to you an equipping language and practical tools for you so your life can improve and change in days, not decades.

In the book you will be equipped with "Transformational Thinking Statements" you can use in your daily life. (We recommend you read these three to five times a day or as needed.) When you use these daily, you can improve your personal walk and relationships. These Transformational Thinking Statements help each of us to be more Christ-like by trading up to the truth with these practical tools. This better equips us to live out what Scripture calls us to do.

UNDERSTANDING PRIMARY RELATIONSHIPS AND HOW THEY IMPACT OUR LIVES

PRIMARY RELATIONSHIPS CONSIST OF SEVERAL ELEMENTS OF SPIRITUAL SURVIVAL

Spiritual Survival is the highest form of survival and relating we can have as humans.

- Relationship with God—The Great I AM
- Relationships that communicate on a feeling level (emotional relating)
- Purpose to our existence—who am I—inner spiritual fulfillment
- Loving—Primary Relationships with others—compassion

You can't survive without a spirit. When our spirit leaves our body, it's called "being dead."

SECONDARY RELATIONSHIPS

Secondary relationships center around worldly forms of survival. These <u>are temporal or not lasting,</u> but the world is focused on these with the promise of happiness which is fleeting at best.

Secondary relating consists of these three areas:

- Physical Survival—oxygen, food, water
- Environmental Survival—money, positions—material things
- Sexual Survival—gender—procreation

Here is the way to understand the order of human survival and relationships. Most of us are not going to run into a burning building to:

- Make love (**Sexual Survival**)—lowest form of relating
- Get a $500 bill off the coffee table (**Environmental Survival**)
- Drink a glass of water, eat a meal, or breathe fresh air—(**Physical Survival**)

But many people will run into a burning building to save a person's life even if they don't know the person—(**Spiritual Survival**).

That's right. We will risk our very physical life to save another person's life. This is the way we are wonderfully made. Why? Because we are built in Christ's image; people have souls. Spiritual Survival—our relationship with Jesus makes total sense why Christ would "die for our sins," wouldn't it?

Christ chooses a Primary Relationship with us, and since we have the risk of burning in eternal flames (hell) He came to save us from burning up by dying for our sins. He paid the ultimate price for our sins. All we need to do is recognize His part of the relationship with us and choose to have a personal Primary Relationship with Him. Pretty good deal if you ask me.

The fact is so simple, people miss this precious gift freely given by Someone who loves us more than even our closest friend or family.

SO WHY ARE PRIMARY RELATIONSHIPS SO IMPORTANT?

When we don't have a Primary Relationship, we are always looking for one. Why? Because this is the way all humans are wired. We need Primary Relationships just like we need to breathe. When we don't know what a Primary Relationship is, we may be looking in ALL THE WRONG PLACES.

- Men and women jump from bed to bed, in and out of relationships, "being unequally yoked."
- People stay in relationships that are unhealthy in the hopes of getting their needs met. That is not Biblically sound.
- People manipulate others to get their needs met.
- People cheat on their husbands and wives to get selfish needs met.
- People lie in order to get their needs met.
- And the lists go on . . . and the sin goes on. And the needs are not met, just more emptiness, more guilt, more shame, more confusion, more anger, and more hurt.

"I am the way, the truth, the life," says the Lord. John 14:6 (NKJV)—This is real truth, because He died for you to have the greatest relationship with you that you will ever have. Then you begin to understand what all this world is about.

BUILDING LASTING BIBLICALLY BASED LOVING RELATIONSHIPS

It's a known fact if you want a lasting relationship with a spouse you need to have a Primary Relationship. I recommend that you read the sections: **Expressive Thinking and Compassion Thinking**. These are the ingredients for a Primary Relationship with those you love, whether they are friends, family, or mirroring Christ Himself, since you are mightily made in His image.

HOW DOES CHRIST FIT IN THIS WORLDLY MESS WE CALL LIFE?

When reading the Bible, you realize that Jesus was a very loving and compassionate person. He was very relational and compassionate. Jesus reflects God the Father's love for us. So much so, He offered His Son's life to die for you and me. This is our ticket to heaven. It's free. All we have to do is ask for forgiveness and to have a loving relationship with Jesus as it says in John 3:16. So how does this fit into our lives?

If a new friend sold his house, and gave you a free all-expenses paid trip around the world, what would you think of this person? Would you think this individual liked you or didn't like you? This sounds like a ridiculous question. Obviously, the person liked you, right? Or here is another example: A young man who is madly in love worked for two years saving to give his future bride a 3-carat diamond ring. Why? Because he loves her a whole lot.

What would you think if you were walking across the street with your best friend as a big Mack truck turned the corner, and your friend pushed you to safety, but in the process of saving your life your friend was hit by the truck and died? Christ is like this friend; He only asks you to have a close Primary Relationship with Him and ask for forgiveness. That means saying thank you for the free ticket to heaven, and also saying you're sorry for your sins. Why say you are sorry? Because that is what real friends do, to maintain a real relationship.

Transformational Thinking Tools—We Are What We Think About!
Based on Romans 12:2

Transformational Tools Are What We Call, "Thinking Trade-Ups"

The Bible is an amazing book. To me it's the greatest book anyone can read. It has so many facets that they are too numerous for me to list. However, I would like to point out it's the greatest equipping manual for your life and the greatest advice you will ever receive in your life. One small area we will focus on is Romans 12:2, which states "... be transformed by the renewing of your mind." (NIV)

Let's take a closer look by using this example: You are in your living room, and you hear a large banging of your front door, very loud growling, and clawing. It sounds like a very large bear. In fact, it's so loud you think that it could be breaking down the front door. Based on this scenario, you are believing something like, "If I open the door I am going to die," right?

Then after about 40 seconds of panic and fear, you hear another sound, people outside your door laughing at the top of their lungs and one of them says your name. You then realize it's your friends playing a joke on you. The fear subsides, and you peek out the window to see your friends laughing hysterically on your front lawn.

Your "thinking was transformed by the renewing of your mind" from fear to relief when you knew the truth. The truth set you free. Scripture says, "and the truth shall set you free." The mind is a very interesting gift we have. When it believes a lie, it sends out a message like fear, anxiety, or depression. People then become "reactors instead of responders."

Let's consider Joe working as a bookkeeper in the accounting department, with his coworker Mary. They both have to balance the books by the 28th of the month.

Joe still believes 3 x 5 = 14. Mary believes **3 x 5 = 15**. What can we predict? Joe's part of the books <u>won't balance.</u> When Mary discovers this on the 27th of the month, we predict Mary will be burning the midnight oil doing Joe's portion of the books because she doesn't want to get in trouble with the boss. We can predict Mary showing up at work on the due date of the 28th with red eyes, looking haggard, and quite upset with Joe. Mary may also have discovered that Joe's mistakes are directly related to his belief **3 x 5 = 14**. She confronts Joe with the truth 3 x 5 = 15. What is Joe's response, "No! It's not, It's 14." Why does Joe insist he is right? Because it's all Joe knows even if it's not the truth, because he has not "traded-up to the truth." He is just defending his idea in what he currently believes.

Many beliefs that we are believing can be counterproductive because we have not traded-up to the truth that would set us free. When we argue to be right or make our ideas, or what we do, an extension of ourselves, we are not living a transformed life.

The following illustrates counterproductive feelings and it outlines the cause (outdated thinking source). This will guide you to the corresponding chapters that follow.

The Source of Your Thinking That Causes Fears & Anxiety

What You May be Feeling Symptom	Cause Outdated Thinking
Anger	High Over Expectant
Arguing	High Over Expectant
Resistant; Opposes Others' Ideas	High Contrary

Fear of Risk	High Self-Defeating
Over Reacts; Overly Personalizes	High Hypersensitive
Disagreeable	High Contrary
Feel Rejected	High Self-Doubting
Indecisive	High Self-Doubting
Put Yourself Down	High Self-Defeating
Has the Need to Be Right	High Over Expectant
Indifferent	Low Compassion
Low Self-Assured	High Self-Doubting High Self-Defeating High Hypersensitive
Shy / Introverted	Low Expressive Low Compassion
Question Your Decisions	High Self-Doubting
Haughty / Prideful	High Over Expectant
Vengeful	High Over Expectant
Judgmental	High Over Expectant
Self-Righteous	High Over Expectant
Lack of Caring	Low Compassion High Over Expectant
Self-Critical	High Self-Defeating
Boastful / Arrogant	High Contrary High Over Expectant
Giving Up Attitude	High Self-Defeating
Counterfeit Independence	High Over Expectant High Contrary

"The Lord is my light and my salvation;
Whom shall I fear?
The Lord is the strength of my life;
Of whom shall I be afraid?"

Psalm 27:1 (NKJV)

NOTES

CHAPTER 2

DECISIVE THINKING

Are You Frustrated by Your Inability to Take Charge and Make Better Decisions?

> *"So then, my beloved brethren, let every man be swift to hear, slow to speak, slow to wrath; for the wrath of man does not produce the righteousness of God."*
>
> JAMES 1:19-20 (NKJV)

INTRODUCTION

Have you spent much of your life in admiration of people around you who appear to be ambitious and successful? Do you ever wish that you could take charge of your life the way they have done with theirs, and realize your goals and dreams?

People sometimes develop counterproductive or avoidance fear-based behaviors in order to cope with life's demanding situations. While these avoiding behaviors may be protective of self at first, if they are practiced often enough, they become ingrained fear-motivators that block oneself from achieving a high level of Decisive Thinking and a more productive life.

Have you ever experienced the inability to make a decision quickly, and felt forced to ask for advice from others before taking any risks? Perhaps you grew up in an environment where others made decisions for you and did not allow you to think for yourself. Do you sometimes fear taking charge of your life because you might make mistakes? Are you anxious about taking a risk or fear what people will think of you, so you avoid stepping out and taking charge of your life?

If any of this is true, then this program is written just for you. The information in this program can help you rebuild your sense of Decisive Thinking, helping you make better decisions in your life. It is designed to provide you with new tools to develop more personal self-control that will help you take charge of your life.

DECISIVE THINKING

Are You Frustrated By Your Inability to Take Charge and Make Better Decisions?

You can better understand where you are right now. Please check all the areas that apply to you in the list that follows:

*People **HIGH** in Decisive Thinking are . . .*

_____ Very assertive
_____ Goal oriented
_____ Strong decision makers
_____ Self-assured
_____ Independent
_____ Take-charge people
_____ Self-motivated achievers
_____ Personable, have high integrity
_____ Action-oriented
_____ Enthusiastic

Biblical Character Examples:
JESUS and PAUL

Strength: This person is assertive and a decision maker. He or she takes charge.

Weakness: If this person has a high Over Expectant driver, he or she may be too assertive.

*People **LOW** in Decisive Thinking are . . .*

_____ Non-assertive
_____ Slow decision makers
_____ Dependent
_____ Passive decision maker
_____ Motivated by environment
_____ Less self-assured
_____ Lower in self-esteem

> "The LORD is merciful and gracious, Slow to anger, and abounding in mercy."
>
> PSALMS 103:8 (NKJV)

HOW THIS AFFECTS ME PERSONALLY

If you scored low in this "Decisive Thinking" exercise, don't panic. This program may be an answer to the questions you have had throughout your life associated with the inability to make decisions and take charge of your life. If you scored high, congratulations! This program can give you great insights into what others feel and experience.

Do you want to increase your Decisive Thinking skills learning regarding how to make better decisions, take positive risks, and be in charge of your own life? Recognize that you can develop these skills and can systematically become more decisive and feel more in control of your life.

What should I consider? How does low Decisive Thinking affect my life? In what areas of my life do I want to be more decisive?

A person's ability to be more Christ-like and be more decisive is hampered by high levels in some of the fear-motivation thinking—such as high Self-Doubting, high Self-Defeat, and/or Hypersensitive. Here is an opportunity to free yourself of any negative beliefs that reduce your Decisive Thinking. You can develop the new skills you need to be more decisive. Often, the ability to take charge involves skills that were not learned early in life.

WHAT DECISIVE PEOPLE KNOW

People with a high Decisive Thinking score enjoy taking charge and making decisions. They may often take risks in making decisions but have an optimistic and self-assured manner of living life. They do not often feel that they have to ask for other's opinions or help in making decisions and they recover from perceived failure easily, should their decisions be wrong. People high in Decisive Thinking are also not overly sensitive to what people say or think about them. They are self-sufficient and are able to lead others, manage projects, and be successful in relationships. These Decisive individuals are good leaders and managers. They are able to be assertive, action oriented, and often thrive under pressure.

HOW LOW DECISIVE CAUSES STRESS

We probably all admire people who are high in Decisive traits and we may feel discouraged by thinking, "I don't know how to be like that. When I was growing up, I didn't have anyone to model decisive behavior."

People with a low Decisive driver may not be able to make decisions easily, leaving others frustrated when they need to know what that person needs or wants. People with low Decisive Thinking find it hard to take risks and normally acquiesce to the demands of others. This can lead to internal frustration and a lack of self-worth, which results in internal stress or even depression. In management levels, the ability to take charge by demonstrating strong leadership skills is important; not having the necessary skills can cause high levels of stress for the manager and a sense of frustration among employees. Employees may complain that they are never able to get a clear decision from the manager, or that he or she might depend too much on employees and not assume responsibility. This creates insecurity and fear in the workplace as employees don't really know where they stand with the manager.

WHAT TO CONSIDER

Has anyone complained about you not being decisive or taking charge when you've needed to? Has this frustrated you to the point of pulling back or withdrawing from challenges because you don't know how to deal with them effectively?

At this point people get frustrated "feeling stuck" and give in to the belief, "That's just the way I'm built." However, this is not true. Being able to take charge of your life and make decisions (your Decisive Thinking) is a learned behavior. A lot of people have experienced increased success at work and at home, as a result of developing this new thinking skill. List a few situations that frustrate you when you are hesitant about making decisions (lack of being assertive) or taking charge of a situation.

1.

2.

3.

You can look for ways to conquer these frustrations by forcing yourself to make a decision all on your own. Recognize you have the ability to make good decisions; you just have to start experiencing them in order to gain that good feeling and confidence. You can systematically develop your Decisive level this way.

> *"Finally, brethren, whatever things are true, whatever things are noble, whatever things are just, whatever things are pure, whatever things are lovely, whatever things are of good report, if there is any virtue and if there is anything praiseworthy; meditate on these things."*
>
> PHILIPPIANS 4:8 (NKJV)

Story of Mary

Mary was a successful personal assistant and a mother of two teenage sons. She and her husband enjoyed family time together and Mary always looked forward to the weekends, even though she thoroughly enjoyed her job. Her boss, Ted, was a successful accountant with a large client base and he was very good to her. At work, Mary was mostly required to keep the paperwork up to date and answer Ted's phone when he was busy. She also managed the billing and worked closely with his bookkeeper. The work was not demanding, but she was always busy.

One Friday, Mary was planning on leaving a little early to get to a basketball game with her family. Shortly after 4 p.m., a phone call came in from a long-standing client looking for Ted and he seemed really angry. Mary told him Ted was out of town until the coming Tuesday. The client said that he had not yet received his tax return, which had to be in the mail by 6 p.m. that day. Mary knew that Ted had completed the papers, but she didn't know where they were.

She knew if she called Ted on his cell phone, he would be angry—he hated being interrupted when he was out of town. Mary asked the client to hold, and frantically looked around the office for any sign of the documents, with no luck. She was really anxious and didn't know how to deal with the situation. She said to the client that she was sorry, but there was not much she could do, and she couldn't see his documents in the office. The client hung up on her in disgust and said that he would contact Ted personally.

Mary was devastated. She left the office and tried not to think about it during the evening. When she and her family got home, there was a message on her answering machine from Ted. He was furious that she had not immediately contacted him, as he could have told her that the documents had to be delayed as they were missing some information. Apparently, the client had not received Ted's email about this, and the matter could have been resolved, had Mary taken charge of the situation. Mary spent the weekend in misery, as she realized Ted was right. She should have taken charge of the situation instead of avoiding calling Ted. She felt like a complete failure.

Examining the Impact

Mary's inability to make decisions, or take risks, was having a counterproductive effect on her life in so many areas. Perhaps this was the reason she had never finished her law degree or dropped out of the book club the past month when she couldn't get along with one person. Mary felt continually tired as she met the needs of all those in her life. Mary was experiencing the negative impact of low Decisive Thinking.

Jesus Is Our Living Example

Jesus was a very Decisive person: He knew who He was and was not afraid to speak His mind even if others disagreed. He wasn't afraid to speak the truth and didn't worry about being "politically correct." This is a perfect example of modeling Christ-centered thinking. Jesus used sanctified common sense. That is factual thinking that is "truth centered" and is honest, without needing to kiss up to others just to feel OK. This is living a confident life, not worrying about being responsible for others' feelings. Other people are responsible for their own feelings.

Jesus Modeled These Qualities

He was assertive, goal oriented, a strong decision maker, self-assured, very independent, a take-charge person, self-motivated, personally had very high integrity, action-oriented, and very enthusiastic. Jesus is the perfect model of how we should live.

THE IMPACT OF DECISIVE THINKING IN INTERACTIONS WITH OTHERS

During the course of a normal week, analyze a situation in your interaction with people (at work, family, or socially) that demonstrated your low level of Decisive Thinking. You can address your observations and record the essence of these interactions.

ASK YOURSELF:

In what situations are you observing low levels of Decisive Thinking in yourself or others?

What are the circumstances triggering me to not make decisions and with whom?

How would I like to change regarding being more self-motivated or being more action-oriented?

How did I let my emotions prevent me from taking charge or stifle my making an objective decision?

How would being more Decisive help bring more joy to my life?

How would being more Decisive impact my relationships with people, family, coworkers, and friends?

> *"Yet the righteous will hold to his way,*
> *And he who has clean hands will be stronger and stronger."*
>
> JOB 17:9 (NKJV)

In order for us as children to learn to be good decision makers, we needed our parents to teach us how to make a decision. Now for others of us, our parents may have made decisions for us or we started trying to "please others" and made decisions based on trying to make others happy and not considering our own needs. If this is the case, we develop low Decisive Thinking. This lack of being able to make an objective decision is not a Christ-like quality and at our core we know this.

In Scripture we are told, "Be strong in our faith." We are encouraged to be leaders. Leaders are able to make strong loving decisions and not be afraid of man. In other words, a leader has the ability to make a decision that is objective and does not worry about pleasing people in order to feel OK. You are already OK because we are built in God's image, and you are encouraged to become more decisive and not afraid to be yourself, becoming more Christ-like in character.

Story of Fred

Fred was in purchasing in the construction industry when he moved out of the area and took a new position as a purchasing director for an electronics firm. He felt out of place at first because he had to learn about purchasing from vendors in an entirely new industry.

Because of his unfamiliarity with the industry, Fred became very hesitant in making buying decisions for the electronics firm. He kept asking others if he should buy certain items. This was OK for the first three weeks; however, his boss became frustrated when some items that should have been purchased didn't arrive for installation at the job sites. When confronted, Fred stammered and muttered, "I just wasn't sure which items I needed to order so I was still asking around."

Fred's low Decisive Thinking emotionally paralyzed him.

People low in Decisive Thinking find it hard to assume leadership in work situations, especially when under pressure. The low Decisive Thinking may be the result of high levels of fearful thinking, such as Self-Doubting, Self-Defeat, and Hypersensitive. The low Decisive person often needs others to take charge and make decisions. This can slow down projects and work production.

People with a high Decisive Thinking tend to be respected more easily by employees and coworkers. These individuals are often well liked because people know that they will take the lead when needed and "make things happen." The high Decisive person will make decisions naturally—they are competent with this skill.

Decisive Thinking is a critical trait for anyone in a management or executive position. The way decisions are made and problems are solved greatly impacts the productivity of any work unit. If an individual doesn't take charge and becomes uncomfortable with making decisions, it can cause frustration and low morale among team members and employees, with great impact on productivity and hence profitability.

> *"A fool's wrath is known at once, But a prudent man covers shame."*
>
> PROVERBS 12:16 (NKJV)

> *"A fool's mouth is his destruction, And his lips are the snare of his soul."*
>
> PROVERBS 18:7 (NKJV)

YOUR PERSONAL DEVELOPMENT PLAN

Up to this point, you have spent some time gaining a deeper understanding of Decisive Thinking and examining the impact of this thinking in the work environment. Now you are ready to begin the process of building improved decision-making skills and increasing your Decisive Thinking.

SKILLS TO TAKE CHARGE OF YOUR LIFE

We can change our thinking and understand that each exercise is a learning process. There are no failing steps in life's journey. There is only failure if we stop moving forward. So, we must prove to ourselves that we can learn beyond the first obstacle. Accept yourself for being human. No human can do everything right! Mistakes or perceived failures are "opportunities" to learn and grow. We learn from these and make corrections, until we reach the goal; this is normal.

AREAS FOR GROWING

1. Start making small decisions without asking for help or reassurance.
2. Avoid critical people.
3. Choose to overcome the fear of what people might think if you make a bad decision.
4. Create an independent thinking pattern.
5. Create positive plans and go after them.
6. Begin to take more calculated risks.
7. Look at decisions in your life that you are currently avoiding.
8. Choose success.
9. Choose Genuine Independence!
10. Think positive thoughts.

Choose to not have a bad day for the next two days, regardless of what happens around you. It's your day—you have control over how you want it to be. Even if you stumble you can get up and run again. Never stay down. Recover, move forward, and never look back.

Decisive–Transformational Thinking Statements
Truths to Set Your Thinking Free

Check all that apply to you:

_____I will make more decisions and not look toward others to make decisions for me.

_____I will practice making my own decisions in a positive, confident manner on a regular basis calling on God's guidance.

_____I choose to learn how to be more independent by trusting in God and not others.

_____I choose to face decisions and challenges with a positive mindset and take reasonable risks.

_____I choose to take charge of situations when I need to according to His will.

_____I choose to think positively as God sees me and overcome obstacles quickly.

_____I choose to conquer my feelings of inadequacy by being more decisive as Christ would.

_____I choose to overcome feelings of failure and learn from them.

_____I choose to be more assertive and confident of myself because I am built in Christ's image.

_____I will be more assertive in a positive manner and reach my goals in Christ.

***Read your Transformational Thinking Statements
three to five times a day or as needed.***

"I sought the Lord, and He heard me,
And delivered me from all my fears."

PSALM 34:4 (NKJV)

"The discretion of a man makes him slow to anger,
And his glory is to overlook a transgression."

PROVERBS 19:11 (NKJV)

NOTES

CHAPTER 3

SELF-ASSURED THINKING

Learning to Trust Yourself / Increasing Your Confidence

Are You Tired of Not Liking Yourself?
Are You Self-Critical and Lacking Inner Confidence?

> *"A fool vents all his feelings, But a wise man holds them back."*
>
> Proverbs 29:11 (nkjv)

INTRODUCTION

Do you find yourself lacking in self-esteem and often put yourself down, not trusting in your ability to achieve goals and be persistent? Sometimes life experiences force people to develop negative or fear-based behaviors in order to cope with situations. While these behaviors may be protective of self, and successful at the time, if they are practiced often enough, they become ingrained fear-motivators that block you from achieving a realistic level of self-regard and motivation.

Have you ever experienced a sense of failure when you don't achieve a goal, and then put yourself down, thinking you will NEVER be able to achieve anything? Perhaps you grew up in an environment where others didn't affirm you or help you build self-confidence. Do you sometimes fear taking risks because you might make mistakes? Are you anxious about what people will think of what you do, or who you are, so you avoid living life with self-assurance?

If any of this is true, then this chapter is written just for you. The information in this program can help you increase your confidence and self-regard. It is designed to provide you with new equipping tools to develop the skills that will help you develop a sense of self-sufficiency and inner confidence.

SELF-ASSURED THINKING

Learning to Trust Yourself /Increasing Your Confidence

> *Are You Tired of Not Liking Yourself?*
> *Are You Self-Critical and Lacking Inner Confidence?*

You can better understand where you are right now. Please check all the areas that apply to you in the list that follows:

People **HIGH** *in Self-Assured Thinking are . . .*

_____ Self-sufficient
_____ Realistic
_____ Determined
_____ Persistent
_____ High in self-regard
_____ Self-assured
_____ Creative and imaginative
_____ Logical thinkers
_____ Responsible leaders

Biblical Character Examples:
***JESUS* and**
JOHN THE BAPTIST

Strength: The person is self-assured, responsible, and self-sufficient.

Weakness: This person may be too realistic.

People **LOW** *in Self-Assured Thinking have . . .*

_____ Low fortitude
_____ Low motivation
_____ A tentative approach
_____ Low self-regard
_____ Low self-esteem
_____ A self-critical attitude

> *"A stone is heavy and sand is weighty, But a fool's wrath is heavier than both of them."*
>
> PROVERBS 27:3 (NKJV)

RECOGNIZING SELF-ASSURED THINKING IN MYSELF AND OTHERS

If you scored low in the Self-Assured Thinking questions, don't panic. This chapter may be an answer to the questions you have had throughout your life associated with the inability to enjoy inner confidence and be more self-assured. If you scored high, congratulations! This chapter can give you great leadership insights into what others feel and experience.

Do you want to increase your confidence? If so, then you need to be willing to take risks, enjoy challenges, and be a good leader. However, you may be afraid to do this. Recognize that you have other skills and strengths that you can use to systematically increase your inner self-assurance.

Self-Assured Thinking relates to inner confidence, not "task confidence." You may feel confident in completing particular jobs or tasks, or do well at certain practical activities; however, this does not relate to how you feel about your inner self-confidence in general.

> **How has low Self-Assured Thinking impacted my life?**
>
> **In what areas of my life do I want to be more self-confident?**

A person's ability to enjoy inner confidence and be self-assured is often hampered by high levels in various fear-motivation thinking—such as high Self-Doubting, high Self-Defeating, and/or high Hypersensitive Thinking. Here is an opportunity to free yourself of counterproductive beliefs that hamper your confidence. Remember, you can develop the skills you need to be self-assured. Often this involves skills that were not learned early in life—perhaps you grew up in a family where positive reinforcement and a healthy attitude toward failures and mistakes was not encouraged.

What Self-Assured People Know

Self-Assured Thinking people basically like themselves and trust in their abilities in life. The reason is that they often take risks in making decisions, thereby learning to have an optimistic and self-assured manner of living life. They have taught themselves to make decisions and trust in their decisions rather than asking for others' opinions. They recover from perceived failure easily because they realize it's not failure at all, just another step toward reaching their goal. People high in the Self-Assured Thinking are not overly sensitive to what people say or think about them. They are self-assured and are able to lead others, manage projects, and be successful in relationships. This doesn't mean they are boastful or arrogant as found in the Counterfeit Independent, Over Expectant, and Contrary Thinking. Self-Assured people are good leaders and managers. They allow their sense of inner confidence to carry them through life.

How Low Self-Assured Thinking Causes Stress

We probably all admire Self-Assured people who are confident, and we may feel discouraged, thinking, "I don't know how to be like that. When I was growing up, I didn't learn how to be self-sufficient or self-assured."

People low in Self-Assured Thinking often put themselves down and find it hard to accept compliments. Coworkers may complain that they find these people frustrating and negative to deal with, as they will never accept positive statements about themselves and won't trust in their ability to live life successfully.

People with low Self-Assured Thinking find it hard to trust themselves and their abilities, so they will avoid risks and normally acquiesce to the perceived demands of others. This can lead to internal frustration and a lack of self-worth, which results in internal stress or even depression. In management positions, it's important to have strong inner confidence. If a manager doesn't possess this Self-Assured Thinking, employees may complain that they can't respect or depend on the manager, or that he or she might give in to people too easily. This can create fear or anxiety in the workplace, as employees can't depend on the manager to take charge and lead effectively.

UNDERSTANDING SELF-ASSURED THINKING IN RELATIONSHIPS

STORY OF ROBERT AND TOM

Robert was a mechanical engineer and extremely successful in his career. He had attended college with Tom, a good friend, and they had kept in touch over the years. Their wives were friendly, and they often socialized together. One Sunday, the families had decided to get together for a casual dinner.

During the meal, Robert engaged Tom in a discussion about Tom's new position at a plastics manufacturing plant in a neighboring town. Tom had been employed as a supervisor of the product design department and, by the sounds of it, was not really enjoying it. Tom explained to Robert that his boss was an outspoken, aggressive, and critical man who seemed to instill fear into everyone on the plant floor, and he was sick of having to deal with employee grievances.

Robert asked Tom why he didn't speak to his boss about it. Tom responded that it wouldn't do any good, as his boss didn't seem to like him. Tom said he wished that he could deal with people the way Robert did. He was just not able to express himself clearly and was inclined to get defensive if the person he was talking to became too demanding or aggressive.

This was also causing problems in Tom's relationship with his boss, not just that of his employees. Tom said he wished they could just return him to the production line, which was where he excelled in his knowledge of the machinery and didn't have to get involved in problems with other people.

Robert encouraged Tom by pointing out his excellent record (even though it had been with several different companies) and that he should "go for it" in terms of developing good leadership skills. Robert was the senior engineer of a large manufacturing firm, where he had been for more than ten years. He too had started working on the production line but had worked his way up over time. Again, Tom said that he just couldn't be like Robert and lacked the necessary skills. At this point, Tom's wife intervened in an angry tone and asked Tom to please stop putting himself down. She also said that he gave up too easily and his lack of confidence had held Tom back from his full potential in life.

Later, when the evening was over, Robert confessed to his wife that Tom really frustrated him a lot, and always had. He said that his wife was right—

he was always putting himself down and made excuses rather than risking anything new. How can Tom build his confidence and be more self-assured?

Examining the Impact

Has anyone complained about you putting yourself down? Has a lack of confidence held you back from fulfilling your potential? Has this frustrated you to the point of your pulling back or withdrawing from challenges because you don't know how to deal with them effectively?

At this point, people get so frustrated "feeling stuck" and give in to the belief "that's just the way I'm built." However, this is not true. Building self-confidence and becoming self-assured is a learned behavior. Many people have experienced increased success at work and at home as a result of developing their Self-Assured Thinking skills, which is a Christ-like quality.

Take a moment and think about a few situations that frustrate you when you are not able to trust in your abilities or doubt yourself.

Jesus Is Our Living Example

Jesus was a very confident person; He knew who He was and was not afraid to be Himself even if others didn't like Him. He spoke the truth and didn't worry about being "politically correct." Jesus was "truth centered" and is honest, without needing to worry what others were thinking of Him.

Jesus Modeled These Qualities

He was self-sufficient, realistic, determined, persistent, self-assured, creative and imaginative, humble, and He was a logical thinker. Jesus is the perfect model of how we should live. These are just a few of his wonderful qualities we need to model in our life.

THE IMPACT OF SELF-ASSURED THINKING IN INTERACTIONS WITH OTHERS

During the course of a normal week, analyze a situation in your interaction with people (at work, with family, or socially) that demonstrated a high level of Self-Assured Thinking. You can address your observations and record the essence of these interactions.

ASK YOURSELF:

In what situations have you observed Self-Assured Thinking in yourself or others?

What were the circumstances that triggered me to not make realistic decisions and with whom?

What would I like to change regarding being more determined or being more persistent?

How do I let my emotions prevent me from having a high self-regard or being more self-sufficient?

How would being more self-assured help bring more joy to my life?

How has not being self-assured impacted my relationships with people, family, coworkers, and friends?

> *"The discretion of a man makes him slow to anger,*
> *And his glory is to overlook a transgression."*
>
> PROVERBS 19:11 (NKJV)

A lot of people are not very self-assured, which is caused by internal fears and anxiety at some level that holds them back from being themselves. That's all the more reason to understand Christ wants us to not be anxious or afraid. So, let's not take things personally and be more Christ-like in how we interact with others.

In Scripture we are told "Do not be afraid." We are called to be more like Christ and His character since we are made in His image. Counter to the way Jesus thinks are thoughts of Self-Doubt, Self-Defeat, and being Hypersensitive, all of which robs a person from being self-assured and gaining confidence.

Jesus was extremely confident and was always able to deal with people in an objective and rational manner. He simply observed other people's behavior but didn't take on their issues. Nor should you, because you are made in God's image.

HOW THIS APPLIES IN THE MARKETPLACE

People low in Self-Assured Thinking find it hard to assume extra responsibility and leadership in work situations. Low Self-Assured Thinking may be the result of high levels of fear-motivation thinking, such as Self-Doubting, Self-Defeating, and Hypersensitive. The low Self-Assured person often allows others to assume control; he or she finds it easier to follow than lead. This can slow down projects and work production.

People with a high Self-Assured Thinking tend to lead employees and coworkers more easily. These individuals are often well liked because people know that they are self-assured and can "make things happen." High Self-Assured people will put themselves "ahead of the pack" and take risks, if necessary, to achieve results. They are not dependent on the opinions of others in order to feel good about themselves.

Self-Assured Thinking is a crucial leadership skill for anyone in a management or leadership position. The way a leader feels about him- or herself greatly impacts his or her ability to lead others in normal and in stressful situations. If an individual is Self-Doubting and finds it hard to take charge, it can cause frustration and low morale among team members and employees, with great impact on productivity and a positive environment.

> *"The Lord is my light and my salvation—whom shall I fear? The Lord is the stronghold of my life—of whom shall I be afraid?"*
>
> Psalms 27:1(NIV)

> *"In God I have put my trust; I will not be afraid. What can man do to me?"*
>
> Psalms 56:11 (NKJV)

DEVELOPING YOUR NEW SKILLS

Your Personal Development Plan

Up to this point, you have spent some time gaining a deeper understanding of Self-Assured Thinking and examining the impact in relationships and in your career. Now you are ready to begin the process of learning how to trust yourself more and building a stronger sense of inner confidence.

Skills to Build Inner Self-Assurance

We can change our thinking and understand that each exercise is a learning process. There are no failing steps in life's journey. There is only failure if we stop moving forward. So, we must prove to ourselves that we can learn beyond the first obstacle. Accept yourself for being human. No human can do everything right! Mistakes or perceived failures are "opportunities" to learn and grow. As you apply each of the following, monitor your progress by writing down situations that occur during the coming weeks.

- Start taking action without asking for help or reassurance.
- Gravitate away from critical people.
- Choose to overcome your fear of "what people are thinking of you."
- Face challenges with a positive attitude.
- Create positive proactive plans.
- Face areas of which you are afraid.
- Rid yourself of needless worry. Concentrate on TODAY!
- Join a group.
- Choose Genuine Independence!
- Learn to accept compliments.
- Reassure yourself. Build your inner confidence.

Set goals for the items in the previous list and track your accomplishments for each.

Self-Assured Thinking-Transformational Statements

TRUTHS TO SET YOUR THINKING FREE

Check all that apply to you:

_____I will look for the good and accept the good in myself that Christ sees and act on it.

_____I will accept compliments, because God made me for His purpose.

_____I choose to see life and others with a new positive Christ-like perspective.

_____I choose not to worry. Rather, I will take charge and handle the circumstances.

_____I choose not to be helpless. Christ has made me, and my efforts can make a difference.

_____I choose to reassure myself and not rely on others to make me feel okay.

_____I will achieve what I can now, even if it's not perfect. Nobody is perfect.

_____My fears won't stop me from my success.

_____I will have more confidence by learning from small risks—realizing I can do most anything I put my mind to with the help of the Lord.

_____Most of what others say and do is neutral; therefore, I will not read into their actions.

_____I choose to have a great day. Nobody is going to wreck my day.

_____I am made in God's image so I can trust in the Lord.

***Read your Transformational Thinking Statements
three to five times a day or as needed.***

> *"I have given you authority to trample on snakes and scorpions, and to overcome all the power of the enemy; nothing will harm you."*
>
> Luke 10:19 (NIV)

> *"Behold, God is my salvation, I will trust and not be afraid; For Yah, the LORD, is my strength and song; He also has become my salvation."*
>
> Isaiah 12:2 (NKJV)

The unwarranted criticism of self prevents us from fully being Christ-like.

"Call upon Me in the day of trouble;
I will deliver you, and you shall glorify Me."

PSALM 50:15 (NKJV)

"You were taught, with regard to your former way of life, to put off your old self, which is being corrupted by its deceitful desires; to be made new in the attitude of your minds; and to put on the new self, created to be like God in true righteousness and holiness."

EPHESIANS 4:22-24 (NIV)

NOTES

CHAPTER 4

EXPRESSIVE THINKING

Have You Been Frustrated by the Lack of Expressive Communication?

INTRODUCTION

Many people have grown up in families that didn't share feelings. If you are from one of these families, you probably have a difficult time verbalizing your feelings. You may have felt like an alien because of your inability to get in touch with or verbalize your feelings.

Have you ever felt emotionally tongue-tied? Maybe you've been in a relationship with somebody who wanted to know how you feel. You would like to explain to him/ her what you feel, but you don't have the words to do it. Perhaps he or she has been so frustrated that they have tried to shake feelings out of you. This causes a very frustrating cycle that creates feelings of inadequacy and you may have just given up and thought, "Well that's just the way I am."

Let's say for example that there is a foreign language which you don't know, like Chinese or Italian. You would probably feel very inadequate around people who only spoke Chinese or Italian. This is much the same feeling that you experience when you are around other people who know how to express their feelings.

This chapter is written just for you. The information in this program can enhance your relationships at home, work, and with friends. It is designed to give you new tools to develop the Expressive skills that your family may not have taught you.

> *"Then Moses said to the LORD, 'O my Lord, I am not eloquent, neither before nor since You have spoken to Your servant; but I am slow of speech and slow of tongue.'"*
>
> Exodus 4:10 (NKJV)

> *"But Peter, standing up with the eleven, raised his voice and said to them, 'Men of Judea and all who dwell in Jerusalem, let this be known to you, and heed my words.'"*
>
> Acts 2:14 (NKJV)

EXPRESSIVE THINKING

Have You Been Frustrated by the Lack of Expressive Communication?

You can better understand where you are right now. Please check all the areas that apply to you in the list that follows:

*People **HIGH** in the Expressive Communications . . .*

_____ Join in groups well
_____ Have a friendly nature
_____ Communicate on an emotional (feeling) level
_____ Are quick to put thoughts and feelings together
_____ Are personable
_____ Are open
_____ Build Primary Relationships

**Biblical Character Examples:
JESUS and PETER**

Strength: The person is friendly, personable, and open with his or her feelings and ideas.

Weakness: This person may be too open and talk too much.

*People **LOW** in the Expressive Communications . . .*

_____ Are non-expressive—can be cool appearing
_____ May be shy—quiet in groups
_____ Feel inadequate when talking
_____ Are more thinkers—or intellectual

> *"With it we bless our God and Father, and with it we curse man, who have been made in the similitude of God. Out of the same mouth proceed blessing and cursing. My brother, these things out not to be so."*
>
> JAMES 3:9-10 (NKJV)

> *"Now you shall speak to him and put the words in his mouth. And I will be with your mouth and with his mouth, and I will teach you what you shall do."*
>
> EXODUS 4:15 (NKJV)

RECOGNIZING THE EXPRESSIVE THINKING IN MYSELF AND OTHERS

If you scored low in Expressive Thinking, don't panic. This chapter may be an answer to the questions you have had throughout your life associated with poor communication skills. If you scored high in the Expressive abilities, congratulations! This program can give you great insights into what others feel and experience. You can use this knowledge to increase your personal Christ-like qualities.

Do you want to improve your communications? Do you want to know how to communicate your feelings and thoughts to your friends, family, and coworkers? Recognize that you have good thinking skills and you can use these skills to systematically become more expressive in your communication.

WHAT SHOULD I CONSIDER?

How has having a low Expressive communication affected my life?
In what areas of my life do I want to be more expressive in communications?

A person's desire to know what he or she feels is hampered by a low Expressive communication. Here is an opportunity to free yourself and learn how to express feelings. Having low skills in the Expressive communications often causes an individual inner frustration by not being able to articulate ideas effectively. These individuals have not learned the skill of articulating feelings because they, most likely, grew up in a family where feelings were not expressed verbally and had no exposure to this skill. By increasing the Expressive communications skills, you can become more effective as a speaker and communicator.

UNDERSTANDING LOW EXPRESSIVE THINKING

Low Expressive Thinking skills are directly related with the development of internal shyness. If this occurs in childhood, the adaptation may turn to feeling "I have to be perfect before being liked or accepted." This is defined as a person who may have "perfectionist" thinking. These people also can make ideas or tasks an "extension of themselves." The reason for this type of thinking is "their personal value or acceptance" is based on how they perceive others accept or reject them, in direct relation to what they produce. This causes a lot of internal fear when in the presence of people, because the shy person fears not being accepted by others.

People who are painfully shy may overly adapt or protect themselves by avoiding people as a way to obviate their fear of acceptance. They may also put demands and "overexpectations" on themselves. Their "overexpectations" often go beyond what is humanly possible at the moment. This happens in particular if the shy person has high levels of the Over Expectant and/or Self-Defeating Thinking.

WHAT HIGH EXPRESSIVE PEOPLE KNOW

High Expressive people are trusted easily by coworkers, family, and friends. These individuals are often well liked and respected. Expressive people express their feelings easily in words. They are very transparent in nature. Expressive people regularly compliment people, coworkers, family, and friends. They generally know how to share on a deep interpersonal level, because they can identify easily what they are feeling inside. Expressive people enjoy expressing thoughts and feelings and often expect other people to do the same. They communicate on a primary level (Chapter 1, Primary

Relationships). They are like an "emotional magnet," speaking with gestures, animation, and enthusiasm. Expressive people are often great public speakers and are usually very service oriented. They are expressive and share feelings of pleasure and positive experiences with ease. Expressive people may feel frustrated and uneasy if they are around someone who does not express their feelings. They have a strong inner need to connect on a personal primary level with another human being and are good at developing close relationships. They are naturally driven to make people contact, even with the coldest of individuals. Their deep inner sense of trust enables these individuals to be effective communicators.

How This Can Cause Stress

People with low Expressive communication skills may not express their needs adequately, leaving people not knowing what the person needs or wants. Coworkers, friends, or family members may complain that they never know where they stand. This may also occur if they are trying to relate to an Expressive person who "needs answers now." Their lack of feedback can cause low morale and distancing in the relationship, thereby causing stress when working in groups, teams, or family bonding.

People with low Expressive communication skill in leadership roles that require people skills may not express their needs adequately. Employees or family may complain that they never know where they stand because they get very little feedback.

How This Affects Me Personally

The low Expressive person often becomes more task oriented. These people may try to show they care by doing things for a person rather than expressing it verbally. The perfectionist tendency can work in their favor. They tend to make a project—the way they dress, or what they say—an extension of themselves, so if it is not perfect in their own eyes, they may not feel accepted. Once the task has been perfected, low Expressive people feel more relaxed.

What Should I Consider?

Has anyone complained about not knowing how you feel? Has this frustrated you to the point of pulling back or withdrawing from communication because you don't know how to express yourself adequately? Your desire to know what you feel may even have been put on hold because you haven't known how to get in touch with what you feel. At this point people get so frustrated "feeling stuck" and give in to the belief that "that's just the way I'm built." However, this is not true. Realize being able to express feelings (your Expressive Thinking and communication level) is a learned behavior. A lot of people have felt a new hope in their relationships as a result of developing this driver. List a few situations that frustrate you when you are not able to get in touch with your feelings.

> "And when there had been much dispute, Peter rose up and said to them: 'Men and brethren, you know that a good while ago God chose among us, that by my mouth the Gentiles should hear the word of the gospel and believe.'"
>
> ACTS 15:7 (NKJV)

UNDERSTANDING EXPRESSIVE THINKING—COMMUNICATING IN RELATIONSHIPS

STORY OF FRED AND CAROLINE

Fred was a computer engineer who worked for a large aerospace firm. When Fred grew up, he spent many hours in the garage tearing apart old radios. He seemed to enjoy being alone and was stimulated by how things worked mechanically. When he got older, he became quite interested in Ham radios. He even started a computer club at his high school.

Fred didn't talk much at the dinner table. In fact, his parents were concerned about him because they never knew how he felt. People often described Fred as being somewhat shy. True, he was a likable person, but he only had a small number of friends. In groups of people, Fred generally didn't say much—in fact, he was more of a listener.

During Fred's years in college, he dated only the women who approached him. This seemed safe—that's what happens when you're afraid and don't know how to communicate. In Fred's senior year, he met Caroline in one of his business classes. She sat in the desk next to him. Caroline was attracted to Fred because he was a good-looking individual, well-built, and very intelligent. Her nickname for him was "computer stud." Caroline was a very expressive and vibrant individual. She was so animated that you could feel her positive energy in any room that she entered. She had lots of friends because of her expressive open nature.

Fred also was very attracted to Caroline because of her lifestyle and many friends. For a shy man Fred didn't have to develop relationships because Caroline already had developed them.

Shortly after college, Fred and Caroline got married. They seemed very happy. After 18 months, when she tried to initiate conversations, Fred's response was usually in one or two words like "Sure," "All right," "Okay," "Yes. I'm okay" "All right! I told you I was fine; why do you keep asking?" Caroline was frustrated. All she was trying to do was to get Fred to open up and share his feelings. She never quite knew where she stood in the relationship. Therefore, she began to feel "emotionally starved."' Caroline wanted to have a deep Primary Relationship with Fred because she loved him.

How can Caroline and Fred connect in their communication?

EXAMINING THE IMPACT

Are you afraid of opening up? Did someone discourage you from expressing your feelings? Sometimes we are afraid to open up for fear of what other people might say, feel, or think about us. In reality, people are not scrutinizing everything we say. Lack of the ability to be expressive really means that the person has underdeveloped communication skills.

We all have a deep inner need to feel understood, to be able to communicate with our coworkers and friends. By expressing ourselves, we can stop feeling alienated. The only way to be close to a person is to allow ourselves to be emotionally available. The rewards are worth it. The more emotionally available we become, the more we can begin to connect with others. Isn't it interesting that a baby is vulnerable, and yet it is cared for in spite of this vulnerability? You may not, however, receive the response you expected because some people don't know how to express close communication and their feelings. Don't let that stop you.

> *"Now when they saw the boldness of Peter and John, and perceived that they were uneducated and untrained men, they marveled. And they realized that they had been with Jesus."*
>
> ACTS 4:13 (NKJV)

THE IMPACT OF EXPRESSIVE THINKING IN INTERACTIONS WITH OTHERS

During the course of a normal week, analyze a situation in your interaction with people (at work, home, or socially) that demonstrated your Expressive communication skills. You can address your observations and record the essence of these interactions.

Ask Yourself:

In what situations are you observing low levels of Expressive communication in yourself or others?

What are the circumstances triggering me to not make decisions and with whom? How would I like to change regarding being more expressive?

How did I let my shyness prevent me from communicating?

Would being more Expressive in communicating help to get over my feelings of inadequacy?

How would being more Expressive impact my relationships with people, family, coworkers, and friends?

> *"Then Moses said to the LORD, 'O my Lord, I am not eloquent, neither before nor since You have spoken to Your servant; but I am slow of speech and slow of tongue.'"*
>
> Exodus 4:10 (NKJV)

As children, we may not have been exposed in how to express our feelings, because to learn how to communicate on a feeling level would require our parents to teach us how by their example. If they didn't know how to express feelings this would leave us with a gap in our communication skills. The good news is we can learn how to express our feelings. This lack of being able to communicate on a feeling level is not a Christ-like quality, and at our core we know this.

In Scripture we are told to "be strong in our faith," and to communicate our thoughts and feelings; in other words, to have the ability to easily communicate in a positive, loving way and be encouraging with others.

Story of Harry

Harry is a manager of a sales department. Tom, the vice president, put Harry in charge of this department because he had been with the company for many years and showed outstanding qualities when it came to bring in cash flow as a salesman. A short period of time after Harry was promoted, the vice president of the company started getting numerous complaints from Harry's sales personnel. The complaints the vice president heard from the staff centered around two points. The first was that staff members never knew where they stood with Harry. They felt confused because they never received a compliment about doing a good job, yet they felt that they had. The second complaint centered on Harry's demanding posture. Harry would appear to be angry and upset, throwing papers around in disgust and generally creating an uncomfortable office atmosphere. The difficulty with this was that the staff never understood exactly what Harry was upset about. What they did experience was an intense wall of frustration when Harry would walk through the office. The staff's response to this was usually one of quiet desperation. Needless to say, this caused extreme morale problems. Some people even threatened to quit because they couldn't take the tension on a daily basis.

When the vice president asked Harry to come into his office, Harry didn't quite understand why he was being confronted. When the vice president explained to him about the complaints, Harry could only say, "Sure I get frustrated when things are not going my way, but I'm not shooting verbal daggers at people. Tom, I just try to deal with my frustration my own way. I keep it to myself." Tom's response was, "Harry, people have to know what you expect of them. They can't read your mind, so you need to express good interpersonal communication to them. Not knowing your feelings, they are going to feel on edge and confused. You see, Harry, good leadership requires that we communicate exactly the direction we want to take people, in order to accomplish our business goals. This gives our people a team spirit feeling and a clear path to success."

Harry's response was, "Tom, I've been a salesperson for many years, and you can't argue with the fact that I can produce income. So why can't these people keep their mouths shut, their head down, and go after the sales? Who needs this stuff about communicating anyway?" Tom's reply was, "There's more than one way to accomplish a goal, just as there is more than one way to land a plane. Harry, if you're on a plane, which way would you rather land it: nose first or come down on all wheels? I think we need to help you with your communication skills because it is obvious that you lack these skills. By developing these professional skills, we can maintain and increase productivity in your department."

Harry went on to develop his Expressive communication skills. This allowed him to make a deeper connection with the people in his department because they understood his needs; his productivity also increased.

EXAMINING THE IMPACT

This lack of feedback on the low Expressive manager's part can cause lower morale, communication problems, and long-range team stress buildup. At the same time, you may experience the manager's unspoken "intenseness" because he or she can't express or explain his or her thoughts or feelings adequately. In meetings, these individuals may have to "go off and think about the topic" in order to connect their thoughts with feelings before they can come up with suggestions or answers. This can cost companies time and money when it comes to getting projects out on time due to delays in making decisions. Remember, these are people who may be trying very hard to be perfect. They feel frustrated wanting to be able to communicate, but not knowing how to do so in a timely fashion leaves them feeling inadequate.

Some people are uncomfortable when asked to express their feelings. They become "withdrawn," or assume a pulled back approach to relationships. These individuals take a back seat in conversations and wait for other people to make the first move. In severe situations they may become rigid and appear not to be open to change. Actually, they are afraid because they feel inadequate. These are some of the experiences of a person who scores "low" in the Expressive Thinking communication skills.

JESUS IS OUR LIVING EXAMPLE

Jesus was a very Expressive and interpersonal person; He knew what message He wanted to tell the world and was not afraid to say it even if the powers that be didn't like Him to say what He was saying. He spoke the truth and didn't worry about what others thought or being "politically correct" in His day.

Jesus is a perfect example of being able to share our feelings in a positive way, without being negative. He understands the need for knowing how others feel in a deep Primary Relationship, and also understands how people gravitate toward those who can communicate on a feeling level.

Jesus Modeled These Qualities

He was a person who joined in groups well and was friendly, He communicated on an emotional (feeling) level, was extremely personable, was very open, and was quick to put thoughts and feelings together. Jesus built Primary Relationships.

Jesus is the perfect model of how we should communicate with others. These are just a few of His wonderful qualities we need to model in our lives.

THE GOOD NEWS

The good news is what happened in the past is just that—the past. You can learn this skill and you can gain a level of communication that can help you in your career and personal life. Think of it as a way to have a life of new fulfillment when communicating with people.

IMPACT IN THE MARKETPLACE

People high in Expressive Thinking and communication can usually think and respond more quickly in meetings because they have more access to their feelings. In contrast, the individual with low Expressive Thinking may need to take more time to just get in touch with what is going on in his or her head and heart. This can take considerable time and effort on the part of the individual, and result in significant delays on projects and deadlines, costing the company considerable losses in time and productivity.

People with a high Expressive Thinking tend to be trusted more easily by coworkers. These individuals are often well liked because people know where they stand with them. High Expressive individuals inform the people they are working with of situations and changes as part of their natural communication skills. They are flexible in situations and adapt easily to change. Their nature is enthusiastic and outgoing, and they usually feel a deep sense of emotional satisfaction when they have contact with people.

The Expressive Thinking and communication skills are critical for anyone in a leadership position to possess. It allows information to be disseminated throughout the organization in a timely fashion. If an individual doesn't possess good communication skills (low Expressive skills) then information may be misinterpreted or not communicated at all, causing delays or putting a halt to productivity altogether.

Inadequacy is born when your tongue can't express how you feel.

> "Then David said to the Philistine, 'You come to me with a sword, with a spear, and with a javelin. But I come to you in the name of the LORD of hosts, the God of the armies of Israel, whom you have defied.'"
>
> 1 Samuel 17:45 (nkjv)

YOUR PERSONAL DEVELOPMENT PLAN

Up to this point, you have spent some time gaining a deeper understanding of Expressive Thinking and examining the impact of performance in relationships and in your world of work. Now you are ready to begin the process of building improved communication skills for your personal life.

Skills to Building Fantastic Communication

We can change our thinking and understand that each exercise is a learning process. There are no failing steps in life's journey. There is only failure if we stop moving forward. So, we must prove to ourselves that we can learn beyond the first obstacle. Accept yourself for being human. No human can do everything right! Mistakes or perceived failures are opportunities to learn and grow.

As you apply the following exercises, monitor your progress by noting down situations which occur during the coming weeks, in which you applied the exercise.

Here Are the Four Steps to Communication

Exercise—Practice with a partner

Share a topic—What is the funniest situation you had in high school?

Practice communication with the following steps—play your role for each step, expressing what is in each step. One person is the talker—the other the listener.

Note: The steps need to be followed by each person's role.

THE TALKER

Step 1: Communicate an idea—"I feel . . . ."

THE LISTENER

Step 2: Listen—mouth shut, ears open to what is really being said.

Step 3: Give feedback—"What I hear you saying is . . . ."

THE TALKER

Step 4: Confirmation—"Yes, that is correct" or "No, that is not correct." If the listener only heard a small portion of what you said, then say, "No!"

If you tell the listener, and he or she doesn't give you back what you are meaning, there is no communication.

So, start over from the beginning—Step 1 again.

THE LISTENER

If you (the listener) get a "no," there is no communication—Start over from the beginning.

Step 1

80 percent of all communication is listening.

Notes:

_____
_____
_____
_____
_____
_____
_____

CHAPTER 4 EXPRESSIVE THINKING

EXERCISE

PRACTICE EXPRESSIVE SKILLS

Identify and express your feelings. Recognize that your feelings exist, adding depth and interest to our lives. Learn to listen emotionally and express your feelings. The more we verbalize our feelings, the more we gain the Expressive communication skills needed for primary relating in relationships. By expressing our feelings, we interrelate and communicate. To express our feelings, we need to learn to connect words to our feelings.

We can accomplish this goal through a simple exercise. Start with using the list of feeling words (next page). With another person, use this list to develop your ability to identify and verbalize your feeling. A more detailed list is found at the end of this book that you can use for your homework.

HOW TO BE MORE EXPRESSIVE INSTRUCTIONS:

Do this exercise with a friend or spouse. Make sure you say these words out loud so your brain can record them to learn to become more expressive.

Your friend or spouse picks a word from the list (on Page 58).

You answer using the following sentence:

Say: "I feel/felt__(feeling word) when_____(this or that happened), especially when_____(this or that happened)."

This is a great exercise over the dinner table. Each person gets a turn.

Homework Exercise —Let's Go Deeper Using Feeling Words

Identify and express your feelings. Every experience we have brings up feelings inside us. These feelings may be strong and exciting or simple and mild, all in response to a particular experience or event. Recognize that these emotions exist and add depth and interest to our lives. Learn to listen emotionally and express your feelings. The more we verbalize our feelings, the more we become expressive. By expressing our feelings, we interrelate and communicate on a primary level.

To express our feelings, we need to learn to connect words to our feelings. We need to observe them to know what they are. We can accomplish this goal through this simple exercise. You can use this list of feeling words to develop your ability to identify and verbalize your feelings.

Choose a word under any heading. (Make sure you say these words out loud so your brain can record them. This is a necessary part of developing the ability to verbalize your feelings.) Go through the list of "feeling" words several times over the next 8 weeks.

a. "I feel/felt _(feeling word) when_____."

b. "I feel/felt (feeling word) when_____, especially when (this or that happened.)"

By filling in the blanks in the exercise with the feeling word, you can improve your ability to get in touch with your inner emotional self and express these feelings. You can now make the connection between an experience and a feeling by the use of a feeling word. This new skill helps to overcome possible feelings of inadequacy associated with a lack of having a low Expressive Thinking. Individuals having a high Expressive skill are friendly, warm hearted, flexible, cooperative, enthusiastic, and affectionate, and after a little devoted hard work and dedication, you too can experience the fulfillment of having increased communication skills. This will help improve the "speed" of your thinking process and provide for more effective communication in your personal relationships.

FEELING WORDS EXERCISE

1. Your friend or spouse picks a word from the list.

2. You answer using the following sentence

Say: "I feel/felt__(feeling word) when_____(this or that happened). Then go deeper: ". . . especially when____(this or that happened)." This connects your thoughts with your feelings in your mind and mouth.

loved	fulfilled	forgiven	peaceful	tranquil	soft hearted
affectionate	special	loving	comfortable	serene	kind
determined	united	committed	private	forgiving	devoted
respectful	humble	cherished	content	appreciative	humility
electrified	enthusiastic	compassionate	calm	precious	open
poor in spirit	meek	righteousness	submissive	repentant	a giver
gracious	helpful	servant-centered	festive	content	serene
complacent	comfortable	joyful	ecstatic	enthusiastic	inspired
glad	pleased	blissful	cheerful	sunny	high-spirited
bright	animated	sparkling	exhilarated	jovial	frisky
self-control	God-centered	jubilant	playful	earnest	patience
passionate	meek	enthusiastic	desirous	high integrity	upright
concerned	fascinated	God-reliant	engrossed	intrigued	obedient
absorbed	excited	curious	inquisitive	loyal	interested
inquiring	approachable	involved	transformed	trusting	united
connected	warm	valued	giving	innocent	relational
creative	sincere	gracious	desired	fun-loving	caring
loyal	enterprising	monogamous	spiritual	forgiving	believer
encouraging	pure of heart	reverent	blessed	soft	non-envious
supportive	thoughtful	wisdom seeker	disciplined	expressive	sensitive
warmhearted	sympathetic	friendly	hopeful	secure	understanding
encouraged	open minded	courageous	confidant	bold	demonstrative
responsive	brave	daring	faithful	organized	fearless

Expressive Thinking–Transformational Thinking Statements

TRUTHS TO SET YOUR THINKING FREE

Check all that apply to you:

_____I will practice "expressing my feelings" in a positive manner on a regular basis.

_____I choose to learn how to be more expressive as Christ communicated.

_____I choose to face my feelings and express them in a Christ-like manner.

_____Being more expressive isn't the same as just being emotional.

_____Being expressive is sharing openly what I feel.

_____I choose to give positive compliments to those around me. I am a Christ-like encourager.

_____I now recognize that it's not "phony" to express my feelings. It's being real.

_____I choose to greet people with a smile and show my Christ-like loving qualities.

_____I choose to be aware, daily, of my feelings, as well as others.

_____I choose to conquer my feelings of inadequacy by being more expressive like the Lord.

_____ I will greet everybody with a smile and a kind word like Jesus would.

_____I will practice my feeling words exercise and do 10 words a day—Put it on my calendar.

_____When all else fails, respond positively with something vs. nothing—get past shyness.

_____Verbal sharing of feels is the deepest form of Expressive communication (primary communication)

_____Sharing feelings comes from the heart—it's a sign of real strength and leadership.

_____ I choose to learn of language of feelings—daily for the next 12 weeks.

_____ Lead people to me by asking positive questions like "Can you tell me?" or "Can you help me understand?"

_____ I need to think about what the person is saying, not my feedback or comeback.

_____ If I am expressing my feelings, I am not being out of control emotionally.

_____ I will think about what I want to express and write it down, then say it so my ears hear my feelings.

_____ I will use positive leads in statements that will diffuse risky communications.

_____ I will learn how to put my thoughts and feelings together and express them to overcome feeling inadequate.

_____ I am made in God's image and that is not shy.

**Read your Transformational Thinking Statements
three to five times a day or as needed.**

"Let no corrupt work proceed out of your mouth, but what is good for necessary edification, that it may impart grace to the hearers."

EPHESIANS 4:29 (NKJV)

". . . be transformed by the renewing of your mind . . . ."

ROMANS 12:2 (NKJV)

"But you, O Lord, are a compassionate and gracious God, slow to anger, abounding in love and faithfulness."

Psalm 86:15 (niv)

"By this we know love, because He laid down His life for us. And we also ought to lay down our lives for the brethren."

1 John 3:16 (nkjv)

NOTES

CHAPTER 5

COMPASSIONATE THINKING

Do You Find It Easy to Pick Up on Others' Feelings?

INTRODUCTION

Some of the most effective people in our society are the people who know the power of tuning into people. These people are very relational and can pick up on what other people are feeling. They know how to respond to people in an effective and compassionate way. Maybe you were raised in a family where you did not have the ability to develop your compassion skills, thereby losing some of your "people power." People who have underdeveloped levels of compassion are often accused of being aloof or indifferent. They lack the skills for caring on an emotional level.

Do you want to be able to show that you care in a new and effective way? Do you want to gain positive responses from people as a result of gaining new people skills? If so, this chapter is a positive beginning. It is focused on the key elements that help people develop their Compassion Thinking skills. It also gives you the most effective exercises that you need in your developmental process.

Like all good things in life, gaining people skills is going to take practice and effort. Now is the time for you to decide to gain the power of tuning into people. Your decision is what will make the difference. By learning the eight effective tools for greater Compassion Thinking, you can begin to have stronger leadership skills like never before.

> "Finally, all of you be of one mind, having compassion for one another; love as brothers, be tenderhearted, be courteous. . . . "
>
> 1 PETER 3:8 (NKJV)

God is the true source of love and compassion.

COMPASSION THINKING

DO YOU FIND IT EASY TO PICK UP ON OTHER'S FEELINGS?

You can better understand where you are right now. Please check all the areas that apply to you in the list that follows:

People **HIGH** in Compassion Thinking . . .

Biblical Character Examples: JESUS and JOHN

_____ Show compassion—are forgiving
_____ Highly perceptive—pick up on nonverbal cues
_____ Are complimentary—encouraging
_____ Like to be involved with people
_____ Are sympathetic

Strength: The person is understanding, respects others, and shows compassion.

Weakness: The person may be too complimentary.

People **LOW** in Compassion Thinking . . .

_____ Appear indifferent or withdrawn emotionally
_____ Are noncomplimenting
_____ Have a low sympathy level
_____ Are emotionally protective
_____ Can be impatient with emotions

> "Be kind and compassionate to one another, forgiving each other, just as in Christ God forgave you."
>
> EPHESIANS 4:32 (NIV)

> "Be kindly affectionate to one another with brotherly love, in honor giving preference to one another."
>
> ROMANS 12:10 (NKJV)

RECOGNIZING COMPASSION THINKING IN MYSELF AND OTHERS

UNDERSTANDING HIGH COMPASSION THINKING

People who score high in Compassion Thinking have grown up in an environment where they were given a message of affection and love. They were treated as though they "counted" just for who they were. Mistakes or errors were seen as behaviors, something separate from their personal value. Thus, these compassion children were exposed to warm and friendly relationships and taught how to maintain and nurture others.

UNDERSTANDING LOW COMPASSION THINKING

People who score low in Compassion Thinking often are seen as cold or aloof. They may seem to show less sympathy for others and are often accused by others as not caring. They can appear indifferent. This often shocks low compassionate individuals because, if asked, their response is usually, "Of course I care," in a monotone voice. Low Compassion Thinking creates a lack of outside perception on a feeling level. These individuals are "thinking" or "fact finding" people, so they don't pick up on the emotional or feeling side to life. This causes frustration in others who try to closely relate to them. These individuals don't pick up on "nonverbal cues."

If the low Compassion Thinking is offset by a high Self-Doubting, a person will need to please others to feel secure, giving him or her the appearance of being compassionate. These individuals also don't pick up on nonverbal cues.

Expecting a person with a low Compassion Thinking to be great at reading your emotional needs can be a frustrating experience. Stress can occur for these individuals when they're facing high social or interpersonal demands requiring them to be 'up' or 'on stage.' Their energy is lost very quickly, and they may also become listless as the day wears on. Situations that require keeping other people pumped up or encouraged can be a drain because the low Compassion person will forget to compliment or encourage. Don't expect these individuals to show a lot of emotional sympathy or to give a lot of compliments. Their relationships may suffer. Without showing compassion to others, they lose their people power. No relational magnetism takes place.

THE SECRETS THAT HIGH COMPASSION PEOPLE KNOW

People who are high in Compassion Thinking operate from the premise that other people are important. They reach out to others with compassion, give gifts for no apparent reason, and live by the philosophy, "in giving you shall receive." The key aspect of people with Compassion Thinking is their practice of reaching out. These people don't worry about when they are going to receive; they know the "giving law" prevails, so they keep giving and they keep receiving.

We all have seen people who encourage others. These people create an environment where others feel comfortable sharing their innermost confidences. They are good listeners and pick up other people's feelings and ideas. They read others well, are moved by love or pain, and show empathy. Compassion Thinking people have a forgiving nature. They recognize when someone needs a kind word said to them and are usually very encouraging and supportive of others. This supportive individual acts like a magnet drawing others to him or her. Family, coworkers, and friends often confide in them. High Compassion people respect the confidentiality of others. They focus on other people's feeling levels and compliment them. High Compassion people achieve satisfaction and esteem from 'relating.' They feel "on track," or "in tune" when they can understand and connect well to others on a primary level.

HOW CAN THIS CAUSE STRESS?

When you put people with low Compassion Thinking in a demanding social situation, they may begin to lose energy quickly. Oftentimes they need to go off alone to gain new energy because people may be a drain on them. This doesn't mean that they don't care about people. However, it's important to realize that being around people for too long a period can diminish their energy.

A person with low Compassion may feel stress because other people expect them to pick up on their feelings. The reality is a person with low Compassion Thinking has a short antenna when it comes to picking up on the emotional waves of others. It doesn't mean that they don't care.

> *"But you, O Lord, are a compassionate and gracious God, slow to anger, abounding in love and faithfulness."*
>
> Psalms 86:15 (niv)

UNDERSTANDING COMPASSION THINKING IN RELATIONSHIPS

Story of Ted and Sally

Ted and Sally have been married for about eight years. Ted works as an assistant manager for a food store chain. Sally works as an executive assistant for the vice president of a software company and is the kind of individual who moves very quickly and is somewhat headstrong in her nature.

One night both of them attended a fairly sizable birthday party for Sally's boss. During the evening, Ted had noticed that Sally's boss's wife Nancy looked under the weather. Normally, she was a lady who was quite talkative and mingled well with the crowd, but this evening Nancy seemed detached. Ted asked Sally, "Have you noticed that Nancy doesn't look very well? She seems to be feeling under the weather." In Sally's hurried and brusque way, she said, "She looks fine to me. Why don't you just relax and enjoy yourself?" Ted replied, "Sally, Nancy looks like she's not feeling well. Can't you see it?" Sally's response was, "She looks fine to me, Ted." About an hour later, Nancy had disappeared from the party. When Sally started talking to her boss, she asked where Nancy was. Nancy's husband replied, "She went home sick. She wasn't feeling well all evening."

This wasn't the first time Sally didn't pick up on the nonverbal cues of other people. In fact, Sally was viewed by many of her coworkers as being indifferent and not caring. Sally continually had trouble "connecting" with people, and this caused uncomfortable feelings to surface between Sally and her coworkers.

Finally, Ted and Sally sat down with a mutual friend and discussed Sally's seemingly noncompassionate nature. It was explained to them that Sally merely had an underdeveloped Compassion Thinking level. They were told that people who have underdeveloped Compassion Thinking usually experience life's dynamics on an intellectual level rather than to experience life on a feeling level. It wasn't that Sally didn't care; it was just that she had never learned how to show caring on a feeling level.

THE IMPACT OF COMPASSION THINKING IN INTERACTIONS WITH OTHERS

During the course of a normal week, analyze a situation in which your interaction with somebody demonstrated your low Compassion Thinking skills. Fill in the information in the list that follows as accurately as you can, recording the essence of the interaction.

Ask Yourself:

In what situations have I been indifferent or not sympathetic to others? What are some examples where I have not been encouraging of others? What would I like to change regarding being more compassionate to others?

How has my lack of forgiving or being cool or aloof to others impacted how other perceive me?

How would being more complimentary to others change my life and influence others?

How would developing my Compassion skills impact my relationships with family, coworkers, and friends?

> *"Then He said, 'I will make all My goodness pass before you, and I will proclaim the name of the LORD before you. I will be gracious to whom I will be gracious, and I will have compassion on whom I will have compassion.'"*
>
> Exodus 33:19 (NKJV)

Jesus came to give His life as a ransom for our sins. This is the greatest form of compassion that the world has ever received. Jesus provides the ultimate example of tuning into people—forgiving them, and providing the greatest example of love, perceptive giving, serving others, caring, and encouragement. All the more reason for us to be more Christ-like in how we interact with others.

You are called to be Christ-like because you are made in God's image.

Story of Bill

Bill owned a small restaurant business. After a short time, he had twelve restaurants. I am certain he was successful for one major reason—his caring. It wasn't necessarily the beverage and food he sold; it was the caring he sold. He always had a kind word to say. When you walked into his restaurant you could experience his motto, "We love to serve you." Like all well run businesses, great leadership flows from the top down. This man made sure that the people who worked for him conveyed the same warmth and caring that he had. In business this is called good customer service. As he trained people to model his warmth and caring, they began to experience customers who responded back in kind. This led to a positive, friendly, warm atmosphere that drew even more customers. Fun energy with warmth and compassion is contagious. This gentleman knew this successful combination. This man exhibited high Compassion Thinking skills.

> *"Now may the God of patience and comfort grant you to be likeminded toward one another, according to Christ Jesus."*
>
> ROMANS 15:5 (NKJV)

Examining the Impact

The Compassionate person believes other people's needs are very important. They understand the great law of life that "in giving you shall receive." This is why good companies and smart salespeople have a giving attitude toward potential customers. Many see this as going way out of their way, but to the compassionate businessperson, it's simply a matter of positive business practice and living within the law of life.

Can you think of great leaders, people who attract and encourage other people? Great leaders reach out. They reach out to shake your hand, look you straight in the eye, and ask your name. You experience their caring energy. How did they rise to the top? By encouraging others. Yes, encouragement. They realized that when others win, they win, too. This self-giving attitude shows they genuinely care. They believe that everyone has something positive to give and they encourage self-reliance. "You can do it." "Go for it." "It's not failure." "Try again." They are truly Christ-like, compassionate people, putting themselves in someone else's place and knowing when to give that much needed word of kindness. People high in Compassion Thinking work from the premise "other people are basically good." Because of this nature, they show a strong sense of sensitivity. They are genuinely considerate of other people's needs.

Jesus Is Our Living Example

Jesus was a very compassionate and relational person. He could pick-up on the feelings of others without them even saying anything. He felt what others were feeling and had great compassion for what they were going through. This is another example of primary relating. Good friends just know how their friends are feeling. Jesus is a perfect example of being able to build strong relationships with compassion and relational skills by connecting to how others are feeling and doing this in a positive way. Jesus was encouraging of others using this primary relating skill. We can be reassured by Jesus's nature of understanding how we feel and struggle in our lives also. We can reach out to Him for encouragement and ask for His guidance in our lives. Jesus is our model. Jesus showed compassion, He is forgiving and highly perceptive, He picked up on nonverbal cues of others, He is complimentary, He likes to be involved with people, and He is very sympathetic. Jesus is the perfect model of how we should treat others. These are just a few of His wonderful qualities we need to model in our lives.

YOUR PERSONAL DEVELOPMENT PLAN

Up to this point, you have spent some time gaining a deeper understanding of Compassion Thinking and examining its impact on performance in the work environment. Now you are ready to begin the process of building improved compassion relationship skills and increasing your "people power."

BUILDING YOUR LEADERSHIP AND COMPASSION SKILLS

We can change our thinking and understand that each of life's experiences is a learning process. There are no failing steps in life's journey. There is only failure if we stop moving forward. So, we must prove to ourselves that we can learn beyond the first obstacle. Accept yourself for being human. No human can do everything right! Mistakes or perceived failures are "opportunities" to learn and grow.

As you apply each of the exercises, monitor your progress by noting down situations that occur during the coming weeks.

WORK TO COMPLIMENT AND ENCOURAGE OTHER PEOPLE

Today, think of someone to whom you can give a kind word. Rather than pulling back out of fear, take a step forward and give someone a compliment. Go out of your way and make someone's day. Do this daily this week.

BE A GOOD LISTENER

Show concern, compassion, and sympathy. Place yourself in the other person's shoes and try to feel the experience he or she is describing. Do this daily this week.

BE WILLING TO FORGIVE, AND NEVER HARBOR RESENTMENTS

If we are willing to forgive other people, we are also developing the skill of forgiving ourselves. We all want forgiveness and acceptance when we fall short of the mark.

"Tune In" to Compassion

We have all felt compassion at one time or another. Perhaps it was seeing a small child starving in Africa on the television. Perhaps it was watching someone in our family experience pain or illness. We felt their pain. We need to tap into our experience of caring. So, let's be supportive and show concern. Look for ways to give someone a kind encouraging word. Look for ways you can show people that you truly understand what they are feeling and let them know. You will be amazed at the response you will receive in return.

Apply this at least 2 times per day this week.

> *"He will again have compassion on us, And will subdue our iniquities. You will cast all our sins into the depths of the sea."*
>
> MICAH 7:19 (NKJV)

> *And when Jesus went out He saw a great multitude; and He was moved with compassion for them, and healed their sick."*
>
> MATTHEW 14:14 (NKJV)

Compassion Thinking–Transformational Thinking Statements
Truths to Set Your Thinking Free

Check all that apply to you:

_____I choose to look at the good in others as Christ does.

_____I choose to compliment those I love twice a day—seeing Christ in others.

_____I choose to see and feel others' needs as Christ sees our needs.

_____I choose to forgive others and live a life of compassion and not being judgmental.

_____I choose to respect others' confidences with lovingkindness like the heart of Christ.

_____I choose to show more caring by verbally telling others that I care.

_____I choose to look for ways to compliment friends and coworkers—being Christ-like.

_____I choose to recognize nobody is perfect and that people are deserving of lovingkindness.

_____I choose to express unconditional love like Christ loves me.

_____I choose to show "compassion" for others in my life.

_____I choose to understand others' needs and show more understanding toward them.

_____I choose to compliment and encourage my family, friends, and coworkers two times a week.

_____I will greet everyone with a smile and model Christ's kindness.

_____I will notice nonverbal behaviors and ask positive questions to understand others' needs better.

_____I choose to show caring and concern more verbally.

_____I will have a humble approach when dealing with problems and life's issues.

_____I will practice smiling (and other loving facial gestures) in front of a mirror.

_____I will practice talking to others in a Christ-like compassionate way.

***Read your Transformational Thinking Statements
three to five times a day or as needed.***

> *"Blessed be the God and Father of our Lord Jesus Christ, the Father of mercies and God of all comfort, who comforts us in all our tribulation, that we may be able to comfort those who are in any trouble, with the comfort with which we are comforted by God."*
>
> 2 Corinthians 1:3-4 (NKJV)

"'For I know the plans I have for you,' declares the Lord, 'plans to prosper you and not to harm you, plans to give you hope and a future.'"

JEREMIAH 29:11 (NIV)

NOTES

CHAPTER 6

ORGANIZED THINKING

Do You Think in a Systematic Manner?

INTRODUCTION

Have you ever felt frustrated by being disorganized? Maybe you know somebody else who is? Would you like to manage your time more efficiently? Do you show up somewhere at the wrong time or the wrong day? This chapter will help you take negative unorganized energy and turn it into a positive, streamlined lifestyle. I believe that people need simple, clear answers. It is an effective beginning for getting the systemization to your life that you've always needed. Like anything else, you need to practice. Now is the time for you to make a clear decision, "I choose to become more organized." "I will work through the simple steps to have a more organized life."

It's very exciting to be able to have control in your life because you get things accomplished. By being more organized you actually accomplish more in a short period because you're focused and operate in a step-by-step manner. Never get into the thought process that you can't do things with your life because you're going to be controlled by your calendar.

This is a false assumption. You, in fact, are the one who's in control of your calendar and in control of your life by what you put in your calendar. Are you one of those people who go through the day and by five o'clock wondered, "What did I get accomplished?" Have you felt bored with your life because you weren't accomplishing things? If this is the case, this chapter can help you. Now you can choose to manage your time more efficiently and accomplish the tasks that you choose for your life.

> *"Let all things be done decently and in order."*
>
> 1 Corinthians 14:40 (NKJV)

ORGANIZED THINKING

Do You Think in a Systematic Manner?

You can better understand where you are right now. Please check all the areas that apply to you in the list that follows:

*People **HIGH** in Organized Thinking . . .*

_____ Good planner—skilled in time management
_____ Organized—everything has a place
_____ Orderly nature
_____ Deliberately methodical
_____ Attentive to details
_____ Has regular routines

Biblical Character Examples: JESUS and NEHEMIAH

Strength: The person is organized and detailed in his/her approach. Weakness: This person may be rigid if he/she is too high in organized skills.

*People **LOW** in Organized Thinking . . .*

_____ Impulsive
_____ Unsystematic thinking
_____ Procrastinating in attitude—easily distracted
_____ Disorganized
_____ Prone to be forgetful

> *"For though I am absent in the flesh, yet I am with you in spirit, rejoicing to see your good order and the steadfastness of your faith in Christ."*
>
> Colossians 2:5 (NKJV)

> "For God is not the author of confusion but of peace...."
>
> 1 Corinthians 14:33 (nkjv)

> "And let us consider one another in order to stir up love and good works...."
>
> Hebrews 10:24 (nkjv)

UNDERSTANDING HIGH ORGANIZED THINKING

People high in Organized Thinking skills plan well in advance. They do not leap impulsively into a decision or an activity. These Organized Thinking individuals set aside a special time for planning before they start their day or a project. The planning stage is vital to achieving their goals. These Organized people like to be sure that they are moving in the right direction, weighing possibilities and consequences that may affect their goals. After full consideration, the Organized Thinking person designs a road map, step by step, to complete and achieve the goal.

Organized people normally are not procrastinators. Other people look at them and ask, "How do you get so much done?" These individuals get so much done because they are committed to a "step-by-step, hour by hour logical plan," a plan that draws a clear line from point A to point Z. Moreover, Organized people are motivated to follow through and complete a project one step at a time.

They gain a sense of satisfaction from completing each step of their tasks. You do not find many Organized people making irrational commitments to projects. They commit only to projects that they are interested in and that they have ample time to complete. Because of their organizational abilities they usually have control over their lives and their future goals.

Highly Organized people know they can accomplish more by sticking to their time schedules. They attend to details and are conscientious about following regular routines.

This organized behavior also extends to their thinking patterns. Organized people organize events into a logical sequence. They do not like to waste time, so they have "a place for everything." When Organized people are presented with a project, they immediately streamline the project. They think through the project with a logical step-by-step plan; every step must count. Organized people are excellent at developing office systems and family schedules, as well as creating long-range plans.

UNDERSTANDING LOW ORGANIZED THINKING

Having low Organized Thinking has its good and bad points. Generally, the person will think fast, but doesn't organize well. Typically he or she doesn't like paperwork.

People who have low Organized Thinking skills have an unorganized thinking process. Their minds jump from one topic to the next as each thought crosses their mind. This unsystematic thinking causes the mind to race, trying to remember everything. At this point, anxiety increases to the point where a person tries to remember so much he or she begins to forget. (The mind can only store so much information at one time, like a computer's hard drive.)

People with low Organized Thinking skills have poor time management skills and often operate "by the seat of their pants." With their mind moving so fast, they become impatient and just react, rather than thinking through a problem.

When it comes to self-development, or other tasks, an unorganized person approaches the task impulsively. These people will seem excited in the beginning but, as the task's newness wears off, their mind becomes distracted from the task at hand, and they become bored. This is why they leave a trail of unfinished projects.

How Can This Cause Stress?

The unsystematic person will think fast and try to keep everything in his or her head in order to "remember" what he or she needs to do. This can cause stress because the mind can become overloaded.

The haphazard lifestyle of being unorganized can cause a person great anxiety. The inability of people to finish what they start can cause feelings of failure. Unorganized people become easily frustrated and often experience a lack of "self-discipline." This person may expend more energy doing tasks repeatedly to get the job done. However, people with low organized thinking skills also can do well in jobs where systems are already built in, for example, bank tellers or postal workers.

WHAT TO CONSIDER

Is your mind cluttered? Do you forget by trying to keep everything in your head? Learn to use a calendar daily to develop a more organized style. You have to stay on track for consistent improvement to take place. So, keep focused.

It usually takes 8 to 12 weeks of consistent follow-up in working your daily calendar to achieve results through developing your organizational skills. Developing this new habit will help you to have a more organized, disciplined, and consistent life.

Is your life a roller coaster of emotions? Are people who love you frustrated with your lack of organization? Being spontaneous can be the fun part of being unorganized. However, developing the ability to think systematically is critical to how productive we are in our lives. When individuals are not organized it can affect relationships, because other issues arise. For example: financial problems because there has been no planning; poor performance due to the lack of a routine; and communication problems because thoughts are not carefully organized before being spoken.

Not having some sense of order in our life can grind on the emotions of a partner. When an organized partner has an overexpectation that his or her partner should also be organized, and this person is not, this can cause tremendous tension in a relationship. This tension can then create distance in relationships. If the energy is focused in helping the partner to learn how to be organized, this can create a positive productive relationship.

This is not to say that everyone must be completely organized, but it's a beginning point to accomplish daily responsibilities and create good communication to solve issues in a relationship that requires being organized. In other words, instead of fighting about what isn't happening, we should plan what can be done to accomplish a task. Then out of respect for one another, move forward in accomplishing the tasks.

> *"One who masters order in their life appears to have mastered time and space."*
>
> ANONYMOUS

CHAPTER 6 ORGANIZED THINKING

UNDERSTANDING ORGANIZED THINKING IN RELATIONSHIPS

STORY OF JOE AND SHARON

Joe and Sharon are newlyweds. Joe has a great job as a manager of a local restaurant. Sharon is finishing her degree in history at the local university. After a whirlwind romance of eight months, they were married.

Sharon was swept away by Joe's dynamic personality and his ability to get things done with enthusiasm and she decided to marry the man of her dreams.

Everything seemed to be going along fine in the first month, but one of the things that Sharon noticed was that Joe kept leaving clothing all over the place, including his underwear. Granted, she was going to school and at home more than Joe, but after a few months of this, she kept trying to remind Joe that he needed to pick up his stuff. Joe would say things like, "Yeah, sure. Okay I'll do it." His success at this seemed sporadic. Joe seemed to do fine picking things up for a week or so, but soon Sharon found herself going around and picking up after Joe again. Slowly but surely "Prince Charming's" charm started to wear off.

Sharon was a meticulous woman who had a place for everything and had everything in its place. A neat and clean home was very important to her. Part of her dismay was that Joe would leave dirty dishes in the sink; as with the clothing, she kept giving him constant reminders only to feel disappointed. After about six months of this kind of behavior, Sharon became furious and Joe couldn't understand what was bothering her because he worked full time and she was "just" going to school. After a huge argument during the holidays, Joe found himself calling his pastor.

Upon their arrival in the pastor's office, they started telling their stories. Joe stated that he was a busy man and had a lot of things on his mind. Sharon stated that she was also busy with her homework and trying to finish her studies and that picking up after Joe was a waste of her time. After giving a profile to Joe and Sharon, the pastor found that Joe was very low in his Organized Thinking skills, while Sharon was extremely organized. It was explained to Sharon that it wasn't Joe's intention to be disorganized, but an underdeveloped skill. "You see Sharon," said the pastor, "Joe doesn't think in a systematic way, he jumps from item to item and project to project in his mind and becomes distracted by exterior events. For example, if Joe starts to pick up his clothing and the phone rings, he will go and answer the phone.

When he is done with the phone conversation, he will have completely forgotten about picking up his clothes. You, on the other hand, being very systematic and organized, will remember where you left off and go back to complete the task."

When Joe heard this explained to Sharon, Joe nodded his head joyfully and said, "Yeah! Sometimes I get so distracted. My mind is going a hundred miles an hour and my anxiety level rises." This certainly explained the nervous energy Joe had that Sharon thought was just his enthusiasm. The pastor said, "Sharon, you can help Joe by helping him to understand how you think systematically when it comes to being more organized. The second thing we can do is to get Joe a calendar and teach him organizational skills."

After the pastor had completely explained how to become more organized, he had Joe and Sharon agree to work on an organizational plan so they could both get their needs met in a positive way.

> *"Fear not, for I am with you; Be not dismayed, for I am your God. I will strengthen you, Yes I will help you, I will uphold you with My righteous right hand."*
>
> Isaiah 41:10 (nkjv)

THE IMPACT OF AN ORGANIZED PERSON'S INTERACTIONS WITH OTHERS

During the course of a normal week, analyze a situation in your interaction with somebody (at work, home, or socially) that demonstrated your low level of Organized Thinking skills.

Ask Yourself:

What situations cause me to be unorganized and how does this impact my life? What triggers me to procrastinate?

If I changed my impulsive feelings and became more organized and methodical, what would be different in my life?

In what areas do I need better time management skills and how would this improve my life?

Does being unorganized make me feel embarrassed or frustrated with family and friends? How would Organized Thinking skills impact my relationships with people, family, coworkers, and friends?

> *"Dominion and awe belong to God;*
> *He establishes order in the heights of heaven."*
>
> JOB 25:2 (NIV)

Most people want to be organized yet they lack these skills and end up being saddled with inner stress and anxiety because of their impulsive unsystematic approach to life. God is a being of order. Look around you and see how nature is organized. This doesn't just happen by chance.

We are called to become more Christ-like and need to embrace newfound skills and how to think in an organized manner. So, let's begin to practice these new skills and be more Christ-like so we can better interact with ourselves and others.

STORY OF MAX

Max had a small business; it was a fishing and bait store. Max spent many hours talking with customers who came into his place of business. He loved his work. He had the best fishing equipment available and did rod and reel repair work. Max was a master at his craft and used the finest materials available.

Max had one major problem—he was unorganized! He didn't finish repair jobs on time, his store was in complete disarray, and he had difficulty in finding parts that he had ordered.

This had a frustrating effect on customers because when they came in to get their equipment, they would get an excuse why it wasn't finished. Now, Max could get away with this to a point because he was very personable. However, his cash flow became a problem even though he seemed to be working harder.

Max's anxiety began to increase tremendously because he was trying to run his business totally out of his head. He never planned anything or wrote anything down. Therefore, he ended up with inventory issues, unpaid invoices, and stress problems. Eventually, Max started drinking more just to cope with the stress of trying to keep everything in his head. What does Max need to make his business better and to have less stress in his life?

Focusing on God's order, His Word, and a wise simplified direction in life are the first steps toward the mastery of wisdom and one's confidence.

Examining the Impact

Do you have a place for everything, and do you keep everything in its place? Some people work in a methodical manner, planning well in advance and seeing projects through to completion. These people find satisfaction in attending to details and they accomplish a great deal in a short period.

Highly Organized people are excellent at managing their time. They consider all the facts before making decisions. They think before they react, so they make fewer mistakes because they stop and think through the process before they begin and put each step into hourly time slots.

When a project needs to get done, highly Organized people don't procrastinate; rather, they define step-by-step procedures on how to complete the task at hand. Do you set goals and accurately plan, step-by-step, how to achieve them? Does your daily routine have a defined plan, a plan you devise the day before? Organized people accomplish more than most people do. They experience less stress and anxiety that is associated with being unsystematic. They have a feeling of control over their lives and time because they approach life using their daily planner. They can think more clearly because their minds aren't cluttered with details; the details are written down.

In business it's important to approach life in a clearly defined, organized manner, setting goals and accomplishing these goals in a step-by-step manner.

Have you ever said to yourself, "I didn't think this through?" "I didn't realize how much this mistake cost the company." "My deadline is tomorrow, and I still have a week's worth of work left, why didn't I start sooner?" "I forgot to write it down on the calendar and that meeting I missed was critical to my future." When coming to your next business meeting, don't get caught forgetting your reports or other important information. Remember, a haphazard approach to life can be fun, but it costs you time and energy and can result in missed opportunities.

Jesus Is Our Living Example

Jesus was a very Organized person. If Jesus is the example of God, then we know He is a God of order.

> *"For God is not the author of confusion but of peace...."*
>
> 1 Corinthians 14:33 (NKJV)

We can be reassured that Jesus and His Father created all of nature, all of creation. Take a look at the order of how the world spins in space, just far enough from the sun that we stay warm. If we were further away from the sun, we would freeze or if we were closer to the sun we could not survive because we would burn up. There are billions of examples both large and small, in both macro and micro ecosystems that work in perfect harmony. Look at the billions of interactions in your body, a virtual factory that repairs itself without you even thinking of it. Our DNA is programmed to do great and wonderful things, a virtual organized map of life inside each of us.

Jesus Modeled These Qualities

He is a good planner, skilled in time management, He has an orderly nature, He is deliberately methodical, attentive to details, has regular routines, is organized, and has everything in its place. Jesus is the perfect model of how we should lead an organized life; these are just a few of his wonderful qualities we need to model in our lives. We are made in His image.

Skills to Become More Organized and Accomplish More in a Day

This exercise evaluates your positive action toward improved organizational skills. Please apply the following exercises in the coming weeks.

As you apply the steps of "QUICK AND EASY WAYS TO BE MORE ORGANIZED" and each of the following exercises, monitor your progress by noting down the situations that occur during the coming weeks.

QUICK AND EASY WAYS TO BE MORE ORGANIZED

I should remember two things:

1. What am I currently doing at the moment?
2. The location of my daily calendar.

Scheduling your daily work and tasks:

A. Use a calendar that has hour-by-hour time slots (e.g., Outlook in your computer or smartphone calendar).
B. Do a brain dump. Write everything down on paper. Clear your mind of all the things that must be done that day. This lowers stress so you can think more clearly at the task at hand.
C. Mark the most important item and rank everything on the list.
D. Put the #1 priority item in the first time slot (Example: 8:00 a.m.), and then schedule the remaining tasks according to their priority.
E. Break the big projects down to manageable size (something tangible you can complete in the time available). Include free time and relaxation time in your schedule.
F. For each hour scheduled allow for 45 minutes of work and 15 minutes for interruptions. A common mistake is trying to put too much into a one-hour time slot. This can create feelings of failure and frustration.
G. Make a map in your mind of the route to take. Example: work, gym, store, movies. Do this in a logical and efficient order. This prevents repeating unnecessary steps, or back tracking.
H. <u>Everything must have a time slot!</u> You must employ self-discipline and stick to the task until it is completed. This allows you to work productively and efficiently. Choose not to procrastinate.
I. Always start your tasks at the scheduled time. This leads to learning self-discipline, not to mention relief. See how quickly you can complete a task. You can make this into a game . . . one you can win.
J. Force yourself to complete the task you set out to do. This gives you the great feeling of accomplishment.

Remember: You control your calendar; it does not control you.

YOUR PERSONAL DEVELOPMENT PLAN

Up to this point, you have spent some time gaining a deeper understanding of Organized Thinking and examining the impact of personal productivity in relationships and in your world of work. Now you are ready to begin the process of becoming more organized and achieving more in a day.

Use Outlook on your computer or smartphone with hour-by-hour time slots. By writing down an hour-by-hour plan that is easy to follow you can quickly see what needs to be done. For example, write down a particular task in the 2:00 slot. You can free your mind about that project until 2:00 arrives. Discipline yourself at 2:00 to focus. Commit yourself to devote the time allotted to that activity. Let go of everything else and concentrate only on that 2:00 task until it is completed.

Plan Your Day Well in Advance

This means taking a few minutes each night before you go to bed, or perhaps in the morning over a cup of coffee, to accurately plan your day. Map out your steps. Avoid any backtracking and coordinate any activities in the same vicinity. This is the MOST TIME EFFICIENT manner. In this brief period, you have a chance to control the pace and direction of the entire day. You are in charge of your schedule!

Choose Not to Procrastinate. Have an "I Will Do It Now" Attitude

This may take some effort, but as soon as you have yourself saying, "I will do that later," STOP and assign a time slot to do this activity. When the time arrives, COMMIT yourself to do the task. FOLLOW THROUGH even when your emotions are saying, "I would rather do that tomorrow." Say to yourself firmly, "No, I am going to DO IT NOW, and the reason I am going to do this is because I will feel better if I do." Once you begin the task, your mind will focus, and you will conquer your desire to procrastinate.

Apply these exercises to your daily life. It has made a great deal of difference in the lives of many others. It will be a positive difference that you are able to experience immediately. The Organized Thinking ability can allow you to achieve the goals of your dreams.

Practice daily using your calendar as a part of your life!
It is a quick and easy way to be more organized.

> *"Suppose one of you wants to build a tower. Won't you first sit down and estimate the cost to see if he has enough money to complete it? For if you lay the foundation and are not able to finish it, everyone who sees it will ridicule you, saying, 'This person began to build and wasn't able to finish.'"*
>
> LUKE 14:28-30 (NIV)

Organized Thinking–Transformational Thinking Statements and Truths to Set Your Thinking Free

Check all that apply to you:

_____I am made in God's image and He is a God of order. I can be organized.

_____I will remember that the more information I try to keep in my mind, the more likely I am to increase my anxiety and be forgetful.

_____I choose to keep a calendar and schedule activities hour by hour.

_____I choose to plan my day in advance with Christ's guidance.

_____I will be more organized starting now!

_____I choose to think before I react. Remember God is not impulsive.

_____I choose to set up a regular routine and stick with it.

_____I choose to live an organized life.

_____I choose to set goals and work to achieve them in an organized thinking manner.

_____Procrastination is a thing of the past—I will have a "do it now" attitude.

_____Do a brain dump—I will get my thoughts and tasks out of my mind and on to paper.

_____Putting tasks in time slotting will free me of confusion and keep me on track to get more accomplished.

_____Prioritize my tasks and put dates and times when I start them.

_____Procrastination is a thing of the past. Do it now for a Christ-like attitude.

_____I choose not to be distracted; I will keep focused on what I'm doing at hand.

_____I will motivate myself with an "I will go do it now" attitude.

_____I will put my thoughts in a time slot as soon as I think about it—I'll no longer hesitate.

_____I will plan my day and week in advance—do this 10 minutes a day.

_____I am in control of my calendar; it is not in control of me.

_____I will use my calendar hour by hour and get more accomplished.

_____Instead of talking about getting something done I will take action to get it done.

Read your Transformational Thinking Statements three to five times a day or as needed.

> "... it seemed good to me also, having had perfect understanding of all things from the very first, to write to you an orderly account, most excellent Theophilus...."
>
> LUKE 1:3 (NKJV)

"So do not fear, for I am with you;
do not be dismayed, for I am your God.
I will strengthen you and help you; I will uphold
you with my righteous right hand."

Isaiah 41:10 (niv)

NOTES

CHAPTER 7

SELF-DOUBTING THINKING

Have You Ever Been Frustrated by a Lack of Assertiveness?

INTRODUCTION

If you are like most people, you'd probably like to have more confidence. Many of us lack confidence because our families didn't really know the secrets of developing personal confidence. Over the years, some of the secrets that confident people have and the behaviors they practice have been revealed. One of these is that they have a strong sense of self-assurance. Self-Doubting causes people from achieving many of their goals in life. You may have felt controlled by people or had a difficult time being assertive. You may even find yourself suffering from lack of inner strength. This can certainly cause us to feel unhappy. Many people with a lack of confidence suffer from worrisome Self-Doubting Thoughts. If you suffer from a high level of Self-Doubt, don't panic. This chapter is just for you.

Most of us prefer to have information in a useful format that is simple, easy to use, and right to the point. This chapter is the result of fifteen years of condensed information. There are Transformational Thinking Statements included which you can repeat over and over again in order to overcome the feeling of Self-Doubting thoughts. You can begin to create an inner sense of confidence. Although there are other thinking behaviors that can affect confidence, you will be well on your way to "Winning the Confidence Game."

> *"Be of good courage, And He shall strengthen your heart,
> All you who hope in the LORD."*
>
> PSALMS 31:24 (NKJV)

> *"But the LORD said to me: "Do not say, 'I am a youth,' For you shall go to all
> to whom I send you, And whatever I command you, you shall speak. Do not be
> afraid of their faces, For I am with you to deliver you," says the LORD.*
>
> JEREMIAH 1:7-8 (NKJV)

SELF-DOUBTING THINKING

HAVE YOU EVER BEEN FRUSTRATED BY A LACK OF ASSERTIVENESS?

You can better understand where you are right now. Please check all the areas that apply to you in the list that follows:

*People **HIGH** in Self-Doubting Thinking . . .*

Biblical Character Example: MOSES

_____ Are non-assertive and compliant
_____ Fear decision making
_____ Have a helpless nature—feel controlled by others
_____ Question their own decisions—need reassurance from others
_____ Are peacekeepers through compromise/ (self-compromise)
_____ Look for approval—anxious about pleasing
_____ Are non-assertive when making decisions and interacting with others

Strength: The person is compliant and a peacekeeper.

Weakness: This person may be non-assertive and have difficulty making decisions while looking for approval.

*People **LOW** in Self-Doubting Thinking . . .*

_____ Are confident
_____ Are good decision makers
_____ Are assertive and action oriented
_____ Have strong self-esteem
_____ Have Genuine Independence and confidence

> *"I will instruct you and teach you in the way you should go;
> I will guide you with My eye."*
>
> PSALMS 32:8 (NKJV)

> *"Be anxious for nothing, but in everything by prayer and supplication, with thanksgiving, let your requests be made known to God; and the peace of God, which surpasses all understanding, will guard your hearts and minds through Christ Jesus."*
>
> PHILIPPIANS 4:6-7 (NKJV)

RECOGNIZING THE SELF-DOUBTING THINKING IN MYSELF AND OTHERS

Self-Doubting Thinking is developed when we are children. Did someone make all of your decisions for you? Were you given the opportunity to develop your decision-making skills through trial and error? Or, perhaps your parents or your older siblings didn't like the decisions you made, and as a result you didn't feel accepted. Their sense of "control" overshadowed your need to direct your life by developing your decision-making skills. This left you looking for approval or asking if it was "okay" to do what you wanted to do.

Let's take a look at how to achieve personal acceptances so we can overcome the Self-Doubting Thinking and increase confidence.

The Self-Doubting Thinking causes a person to feel responsible for other people's thoughts and feelings. People feel guilty or selfish if they put themselves first. Is this right? People high in the Self-Doubting Thinking give in, often to the point of selflessness. These people find themselves not knowing who they are. This is caused, usually, by being afraid to risk saying what they want. By saying what you want and need, you begin to discover more about who you are. It is not selfish to have your own needs met, as long as you consider the needs of others in the process.

A workable compromise (a solution both people can live with) can be a good solution. Everyone wins this way. People high in Self-Doubting Thinking undergo a great deal of self-questioning. They are usually so concerned about pleasing other people that they may compromise their own values and give in to others' wants. They are constantly looking to be reassured that their decisions are correct, or that the audience is pleased with their decisions or comments. This is not Christ-like thinking; remember, you are made in God's image.

UNDERSTANDING HIGH SELF-DOUBTING THINKING

People high in Self-Doubting Thinking make statements like, "I don't care," when asked what they would like to do. They allow others to make decisions for them so they "play it safe," by making sure they are pleasing and not offending the other individual. Self-Doubting Thinking detracts from a person's internal confidence. If we were to make a comparison to an automobile, confidence is the accelerator and Self-Doubting Thinking is most definitely the brake. Can you imagine driving down the road with one foot on the accelerator and one foot on the brake? You would feel the stress of the experience and get nowhere fast. Some people worry extensively, or find they undergo a lot of Self-Doubt. "Am I smart enough?" "Can I measure up?" "Am I good enough?" "I am afraid of failing." "Will people like me if I am myself?" People high in Self-Doubting Thinking allow themselves to be followers. Sometimes they even say that "it doesn't really matter." Underneath this follower's disposition is fear; fear that they will not be accepted or of displeasing others.

Do You Feel Helpless?

If so, ask yourself, "What creates this helpless attitude?" The mind can follow that course of thinking; however, you may need to create a new attitude: "I choose not to be helpless; it's my effort that will make the difference." Confidence develops as a result of daily self-assurance and prayer.

How This Can Cause Stress

People with high Self-Doubting Thoughts usually give in so much that, finally, they feel exasperated and explode. They then feel guilty for hurting someone and go back to giving in. Thus, the cycle starts all over.

True, when we are deliberately rude, impolite, negative, and hurtful, we are responsible. However, there is nothing selfish or irresponsible about expressing your needs in a polite and cordial manner. If we learn to express our needs as they arise, we will defuse the volcano from later eruption. Once again, give another person credit. Let him or her surprise you by meeting your needs. It's your effort that makes the difference.

Usually persons with high levels of Self-Doubting Thinking appear pleasant; if it's a primary way of thinking, it can result in subservient victim, or non-assertive, behavior. These individuals need to please others to overcome inner fears of rejection. This gnawing fear causes a lot of internal anxiety and stress. Stress can develop because the person with a high Self-Doubting Thought won't speak up when something bothers him or her. These people give a lot of nonverbal hints, expecting others to pick up on these signals. If another person is not lucky enough to pick up on these hidden expectations, usually the person with high Self-Doubting Thoughts gets his or her feelings hurt easily and may feel rejected when no one is actually rejecting him or her. Such a situation has a tremendous effect on work and home relationships. In the work environment, the person with high Self-Doubting Thinking may even stay at home sick rather than face coworkers, yet they may not risk seeking another job out of fear of being rejected.

> *"The wicked flee when no one pursues, But the righteous are bold as a lion."*
>
> PROVERBS 28:1 (NKJV)

UNDERSTANDING SELF-DOUBTING THINKING IN RELATIONSHIPS

STORY OF BILL AND JUDY

Bill and Judy had been married for years. It was Bill's first marriage and Judy was a very loving, mild mannered person. Bill was a fairly strong person who was the president of his own small software company.

Judy worked as a receptionist at a local law firm. Bill was very busy with his business and had to make lots of decisions and wear lots of hats, because it was a small start-up company. Frequently Bill would ask Judy out for dates and continue the courtship because he wanted to keep his marriage alive. As time went on (because Bill wanted to please Judy), he would always ask Judy, "Where would you like to go tonight?" Judy's reply was always the same, "Oh, I don't know, wherever you'd like to go." After a lengthy period of time Bill would say to Judy, "Look, I really want to take you where you'd like to go." Judy's reply again would be very similar. She would say in frustration, "Bill, you always ask me that, just tell me where we're going."

Slowly the relationship changed, and it wasn't as strong as it used to be. When speaking with a mutual friend, Bill presented the problem this way, "You know, I'm becoming more and more frustrated in our relationship because Judy never makes a decision. It doesn't seem to matter whether I take her out to a show or to dinner. It got so bad that even when it came to wallpaper for our bedroom I never knew where she stood. Then, every once in a while, Judy blows up for no apparent reason and accuses me of making all kinds of decisions for her. I am really frustrated with this cycle." Judy's response was, "I know I don't make decisions. I'm afraid that if I make a decision it may not be the right one."

After talking for some time, it was discovered that Judy had high levels of Self-Doubting Thoughts. Judy complained that she had low self-esteem that affected her confidence. Their friend explained to Bill and Judy that they should work together in developing Judy's self-respect. It was suggested that when it came to making decisions, Bill should give Judy two options at a time and then wait for Judy to make a decision. After doing this for several months, Judy began to recognize that even if she did make a wrong decision she could always go back and correct it. This improved her self-respect and Bill began to respect her more, because he knew where Judy stood. Judy became less frustrated because she took more responsibility for the things in life that she wanted. This enhanced the relationship greatly because Judy developed her confidence level and Bill regained his attraction to her.

> *"But Jesus did not commit Himself to them, because He knew all men, and had no need that anyone should testify of man, for He knew what was in man."*
>
> JOHN 2:24-25 (NKJV)

Examining the Impact

A by-product of Self-Doubting Thinking is insecurity, timidity, anxiety, and worry. Nothing productive ever comes from worrying. Have you ever known anything in your life that was produced by worry, other than stress, anxiety, or fear? Worry is a destructive, useless emotion. We can choose not to worry if we are confronted with an unsettling situation, and spend our energies correcting or handling the circumstance. We never add one day to our lives by worry.

People with high Self-Doubting Thinking may feel ineffective, helpless, and controlled by other people because they are repeatedly compromising their own feelings and values since they are too afraid to speak up and express themselves. They then may feel angry toward friends, family, or coworkers. They do not verbalize this, however, because they are afraid of displeasing others. Sometimes these individuals will withdraw, causing internal anxiety, pressure, stress, and sometimes depression.

When asked, "What's wrong?" they will comment, "Nothing," but something is wrong. People high in Self-Doubting Thinking may constantly worry about how others view them. They never really experience the joys of accomplishment on their own because they need reassurance by continually asking for help. They may not seek to accomplish things on their own out of fear of doing it wrong. They are constantly looking over their shoulders wondering what other people are thinking.

People with high Self-Doubting Thoughts usually give in so much that, finally, they feel exasperated. They then feel guilty for hurting someone and go back to giving in. Thus, the cycle starts all over. The high Self-Doubting Thinking takes away from an individual's feeling of personal value. High Self-Doubting Thinking also results in a sense of insecurity and lack of self-assurance.

Does this sound at all familiar?
If so, high Self-Doubting Thoughts may be haunting your life.

Jesus Is Our Living Example

Jesus was a very decisive and confident person; He knew who He was and was not afraid to speak His mind and not worry if people thought He was OK. He was just Himself without Self-Doubt, and he did not have a need for reassurance. He wasn't afraid to speak the truth and didn't worry about being "politically correct."

This is a perfect example of modeling a Christ-like thinking. Jesus used common sense. That is factual thinking that is "truth centered," honest, and without needing to please others just to feel OK. This is living a joy-filled life, not worrying about being overly responsible for other people's feelings. Other people are responsible for their own feelings.

Jesus Modeled These Qualities

He made great decisions, was strong natured, never felt controlled by others, and didn't need reassurance from anyone to feel OK about Himself. He was not self-compromising and didn't worry about pleasing others because He didn't need approval from others. Jesus is the perfect model of how we should live, especially regarding looking for approval from people. We should only look for approval from our heavenly father where it really counts. These are just a few of His wonderful qualities we need to model in our lives.

Relationships

People high in Self-Doubting Thinking are afraid to express their own ideas. They are afraid of having their ideas or needs rebuffed. They tend to make their ideas and opinions an extension of themselves. Do you sometimes give in to what others feel or want because of the need to please them in order to feel secure within yourself? Some people sacrifice their own needs because they want their significant other to love and accept them. When taken to the extreme, a person may feel almost desperate for attention or reassurance. This can drive people away because it has a suffocating impact on the relationship.

When a friend or coworker doesn't accept the idea or opinion of a person with high Self-Doubting Thoughts, he or she feels rejected. As a result, this person does not share his or her ideas freely, and instead withdraws into self-criticism. We see this happening in relationships when the partner who has high Self-Doubting Thinking packs up and leaves one day for no apparent reason, leaving a partner who is confused and not knowing why the relationship failed. The reason is the person with the Self-Doubting Thoughts kept sandbagging—feeling hurt and rejected, never risking stating how he or she really felt.

A high level of Self-Doubting Thinking prevents a person from making decisions. This often stops productive communication. Remember to give yourself permission to speak your mind. This can prevent long-range communication problems and may even save your relationships. People don't want to be in a position of having to read your mind. Most people are very interested in your ideas. Learn to speak up without fear of personal rejection.

We must understand that people don't mind when we say "no." People who love us are interested in our needs. Give other people a little credit for being interested in your needs. Imagine this situation. You invite a friend to the movies, and she agrees to go, but in a reluctant manner. While at the movies, her mind seems to be somewhere else; she doesn't say much. After the movie you go out for coffee and begin to discuss the show. Your friend seems a little uneasy, even frustrated.

"What's wrong?" you ask. "I really didn't want to go to that movie tonight," she blurts. "I went because you wanted to go." Have you been in a situation like this? Would you have wanted your friend to tell you what she really wanted to do?

Most of us don't want to put anyone through pain or unhappiness. We can now learn to say what we think and need. We can start by saying things like, "I would rather not go to this movie. I don't like violent movies. I prefer comedies." Or "I would like to go to the movie, but I have another commitment." When we accept situations that are uncomfortable for us, no one benefits. We do not get what we want out of life and it makes our friends responsible for our behavior and feelings. We, as people, care about each other and want to share activities that are mutually enjoyable. We want friends to be responsible for their own feelings and needs. It makes for a freer, more enjoyable, happier relationship.

THE IMPACT OF SELF-DOUBTING THINKING IN INTERACTIONS WITH OTHERS

During the course of a normal week, analyze a situation in your interaction with somebody (at work, family, or socially) that demonstrated your Self-Doubting Thinking patterns.

Ask Yourself:

What situations are causing me to have Self-Doubt and question myself? When do I compromise myself and give in to others by not speaking up?

What would I like to change if I quit questioning my own decisions?

How do I let my Self-Doubting Thoughts overrule sound judgment? How is this being counterproductive in my interactions with people?

How does looking for approval from others make me feel down or depressed and even prevent me from feeling happy or having inner joy or peace?

How is Self-Doubting Thinking impacting my relationships with people, family, coworkers, and friends?

> *"Fear of Man will prove to be a snare, but whoever trust in the LORD is kept safe. . . ."*
>
> PROVERBS 29:25 (NKJV)

A lot of people are people pleasers. They feel they have to please others in order for them to feel OK about themselves. This fearful thinking holds most people back in some form from being themselves. All the more reason to understand that Christ wants us to not have a fear of man or fear of displeasing others. It is OK to be nice and kind to others. Love your neighbor as yourself. So, let's be more Christ-like in how we interact with others.

In Scripture we are told "do not be afraid." We are not made to agree just for the sake of pleasing someone else. Jesus was extremely confident and was always in an observation mode and kept things that people said and did neutral. He simply watched their behavior but didn't take on their issues. Nor should you because you are made in God's image. So, speak up and express your thoughts and feelings. Your thoughts are just as important as others'—remember to speak up with a servant's heart as Christ would.

THE STORY OF LARRY

Larry started a new job as a customer service representative for an electronic store. He received a call from a customer complaining that he hadn't received his computer hard drive. In looking at the store database, Larry noticed that the store computer showed that the customer had received credit for his hard drive. The customer said to Larry, "No, I left my hard drive to be repaired and your company said they would call when it was repaired." Larry insisted that the customer was wrong because the store computer showed that it was a credit.

This made the customer furious. The customer retorted, "I need my hard drive back. It has vital information on it. It was a repair." Larry's response was, "Let me check." He put the customer on hold, made little effort to look for the hard drive, picked up the phone again, and said, "I'm sorry there is no hard drive under your name." The customer said, "What are you going to do about this?" Larry responded, "There is nothing I can do about it."

There were avenues Larry could have explored if he would have taken charge and made some strong decisions. This would have required Larry taking action to seek a fast solution to the customer's problem. But Larry suffered from high levels of Self-Doubting Thinking He was anxious about pleasing the customer, but his non-assertive, helpless feelings prevented him from moving forward in a timely fashion to correct the customer's problem.

The customer, being very assertive, drove 25 miles to the store only to find another person like Larry who couldn't seem to make a decision either. The customer finally walked around the store until he found somebody who was assertive and a strong decision maker. He explained his dilemma to a supervisor in another department. The supervisor couldn't believe his ears. He walked the customer over to the service department and told them to correct the customer's problem immediately.

People who have a high level of Self-Doubting Thinking tend to be overlooked for promotions because of their inability to make a decision even when common sense tells them they should. How much do you think this costs businesses every year?

Examining the Impact

People high in Self-Doubting Thinking fear asserting themselves. They fear moving out of the "norm" and expressing ideas. Therefore, they rob themselves of the satisfaction that comes from expressing themselves, taking a risk, and realizing, "My ideas have value!" They do not experience the success of personal initiative.

These individuals may ask for advice even when they are completely competent people. People high in Self-Doubting Thinking avoid making decisions and rely on others for direction. They do this to gain approval. The problem is, by asking for advice when it isn't really needed, they are discounting their own good judgment. This adds one more blow to their self-esteem and lowers their personal well-being.

People who are high in Self-Doubting Thoughts tend to be followers rather than leaders. The word "peacekeeper" describes these individuals. They compromise their beliefs to keep peace. Maybe you have found yourself accepting situations you consider personally unfair because you would rather not risk asserting your opinion or idea.

Have you ever experienced feelings of weakness, or helplessness? Has this resulted in allowing your feelings to be controlled by other people at your job? Do you sometimes give in to what others feel or want because of your need to please them to feel secure about yourself or have a driving need for approval?

People with high Self-Doubting Thinking find themselves apologizing unnecessarily even though they haven't done anything wrong. This creates a negative cycle because they worry about what other people might be thinking of them or of their behavior. It's more difficult to get promoted if a boss senses you don't make decisions easily.

Self-Doubting Thinking gets in the way of confidence building. We need to move forward to build greater self-assurance. But the Self-Doubting Thinking keeps waving a red flag that says, "You might fail, you might not make the right decision the first time!" Then we put on the brakes. We have to understand that people often don't make the right decision the first time.

Trust yourself and don't always ask for help if you know the common sense answers. You often won't need someone to reassure you if you take risks more often. Choose to do things on your own, and prove to yourself that you can do the task; this will help you gain more self-confidence. Understand that others are not out to judge you. Even if someone was, it really could be the other critical person's problem. Remember, you must be responsible for your own behavior and do everything to the best of your ability. Have dignity in your efforts.

> *"These things I have spoken to you, that in Me you may have peace. In the world you will have tribulation; but be of good cheer, I have overcome the world."*
>
> JOHN 16:33 (NKJV)

YOUR PERSONAL DEVELOPMENT PLAN

Up to this point, you have spent some time gaining a deeper understanding of Self-Doubting Thinking by examining the impact of individual productivity and building relationships. Now you are ready to begin the process of building increased Self-Assurance and overcoming Self-Doubting Thinking.

SKILLS TO INCREASE CONFIDENCE BY OVERCOMING SELF-DOUBTING THOUGHTS

We can change our thinking and understand that each step is a learning process. There are no failing steps in life's journey. There is only failure if we stop moving forward. So, we must prove to ourselves that we can learn beyond the first obstacle. Accept yourself for being human. No human can do everything right! Mistakes or perceived failures are "opportunities" to learn and grow. Go out into the world, make some decisions, and watch your confidence increase!

- Your first decision toward improved interaction with others is to apply the following exercises in the coming weeks.
- As you apply each of the following exercises, monitor your progress by noting and writing down situations that occur during the coming weeks.

Learn to speak up for yourself by expressing your desires, needs, and feelings. People want to know our ideas and desire our participation—don't rob them of that gift. Exchanging ideas, needs, and feelings enriches all our lives. We have a lot to offer and we can discover this by learning to speak up. Don't make your ideas an extension of yourself. You are much more than your ideas. You are made in God's image.

- This week take a risk and speak up more when talking to others.
- Be aware of what has actually happened when you feel you have compromised yourself.

Ask yourself, "Do you feel compromised?" What could you have said differently to prevent this? Act on it rather than hoping people will read your mind to meet your needs. You need to take a deep breath, pleasantly clarify yourself, and say what you want. You may be pleasantly surprised.

As you gain confidence in your ability to handle more responsibility, you can gradually add more. The continual increasing of responsibility will make life more enjoyable. You'll find that responsibilities aren't really the threats that you once thought they were. Conquering responsibilities builds self-assurance, increases confidence, and helps you feel good about yourself. We must recognize that people are not out to pounce on us. They need acceptance also. Who knows, maybe their Self-Doubting Thinking is higher than yours. When observing others, we will probably feel less threatened. Take on more "selected" responsibility this week without asking for permission or reassurance from others. (Do this three times this week.)

> *Choose to overcome the fear of "what people might think" if you express your needs.*

Other people are not judging us the way we might think. If they are, recognize they're among those critical people who are unhappy about everything, which is not your problem.

> *Practice this at least three times this week. Record your results.*

> *Start taking on small responsibilities without asking for help or reassurance from others.*

Summary

A key behavior to develop is seeing your worth as a person is separate from your behavior or your ideas. We have our own personal, intrinsic value. Who we are is made up of qualities like kindness, loving, caring, loyalty, and so on, and nobody can take these qualities away from us. Your value is made in God's image and there's only one you. As you adopt new thoughts in your life you can have the confidence you've been looking for. You can overcome Self-Doubting Thoughts and have the vitality and the experience of confidence that will carry you through life.

> *"Therefore, I say to you, do not worry about your life, what you will eat or what you will drink; nor about your body, what you will put on. Is not life more than food and the body more than clothing?"*
>
> MATTHEW 6:25 (NKJV)

Self-Doubting Thinking–Transformational Thinking Statements Truths to Set Your Thinking Free

Check all that apply to you:

_____I'm responsible for my own feelings and actions. Likewise, other people are responsible for theirs. This is a Christ-like quality.

_____It's not selfish to get my own needs met, as long as I'm considering others' needs in the process. I am a new person in Christ.

_____Worry is a useless emotion. I will trust in the Lord to guide me.

_____I choose to decide. If it's not right the first time, then I can change my decision.

_____I choose to express my needs and feelings and recognize that others will respect me for this. Seek the mind of Christ.

_____I choose not to be helpless. My efforts will make a difference with God's guidance.

_____I choose to reassure myself and not rely on others to make me feel okay.

_____I choose to not feel rejected if someone has a different idea than mine.

_____My ideas and who I am are not the same. People may not accept my ideas, but they still accept me. Therefore, I do not need to convince others to my ideas nor give up my ideas in order to be accepted. Christ accepts me as a human with faults.

_____I choose to not make projects, ideas, or tasks an extension of myself.

_____It's okay to express my idea and not be offended if somebody doesn't agree with me. It's just an idea, not my personal value. My value is based on my God-given gifts.

_____I'm not going to measure myself by my behavior, title, or what I do.

_____I will trust in God for all things.

_____Confrontation does not mean my ideas are rejected.

_____When I know who I am, I am in the Lord and feel less vulnerable.

_____I will be more assertive in my decision making, asking God for guidance.

_____I realize that my thoughts matter just as much as everyone else's.

_____I choose not to hesitate with self-motivation and reassure myself through Christ.

_____I choose not to second-guess myself, and I choose to motivate myself with an "I will go do it now" attitude.

Read your Transformational Thinking Statements three to five times a day or as needed.

> *"Therefore, though I might be very bold in Christ to command you what is fitting.. . . ."*
>
> PHILEMON 1:8 (NKJV)

"The fear of the Lord is the beginning of knowledge,
But fools despise wisdom and instruction."

PROVERBS 1:7 (NKJV)

"Therefore humble yourselves under the mighty
hand of God, that He may exalt you in due time,
casting all your care upon Him,
for He cares for you."

1 PETER 5:6-7 (NKJV)

NOTES

CHAPTER 8

OVER EXPECTANT THINKING

Have You Ever Thought of Yourself as Being Controlling?

INTRODUCTION

Many of us have either attended or heard about seminars on how to deal with "difficult people." One of the foremost characteristics of a difficult person is his or her Over Expectant Thinking. This type of attitude creates lots of frustration for people who work or live around these people. Family members who live with this sort of person complain about the constant frustration of never being able to live up to the demanding expectations placed upon them. They state how they are always afraid that the Over Expectant Thinking person would start to get angry if he or she didn't get his or her way.

How do we deal with these difficult people? What goes on in their head? Are they making other people's lives miserable on purpose or are they just out of control themselves? How can we understand them? How can we prevent ourselves from feeling put down?

Discovering Genuine Independence vs. Counterfeit Independence

> *"The discretion of a man makes him slow to anger, and his glory is to overlook a transgression."*
>
> Proverbs 19:11 (NKJV)

> *"A fool vents all his feelings, but a wise man holds them back."*
>
> Proverbs 29:11 (NKJV)

OVER EXPECTANT THINKING

Have You Ever Thought of Yourself as Being Controlling?

You can better understand where you are right now. Please check all the areas that apply to you in the list that follows:

*People **HIGH** in Over Expectant Thinking . . .*

_____ Have expectations beyond what can realistically be produced at the moment
_____ Are judgmental of self or others and easily annoyed
_____ Have a haughty attitude
_____ Are very self-critical
_____ Have "excessive expectations"
_____ Are demanding of self or others
_____ Can be unyielding in their opinion
_____ Feel insecure when not in control
_____ Are more likely to be disagreeable
_____ Are argumentative and/or self-righteous
_____ Have the need to be right
_____ Have difficulty admitting an error
_____ Have out of control emotions that may overcome their sound intellect

Biblical Character Example: SAUL

Strength: Good closer in sales positions

Weakness: Too demanding, critical, argumentative, and judgmental

*People **LOW** in Over Expectant Thinking . . .*

_____ Are more compliant and understanding
_____ Are humble
_____ Are cooperative and display realistic expectations
_____ Deal with others in a positive manner
_____ Are generally more forgiving

> *"He mocks proud mockers but shows favor to the humble and oppressed.
> The wise inherit honor, but fools get only shame."*
>
> Proverbs 3:34-35 (NIV)

> *"Do you know that the unrighteous will not inherit the kingdom of God? . . .
> but you were washed, but you were sanctified, but you were justified in the
> name of the Lord Jesus and by the Spirit of our God."*
>
> 1 Corinthians 6:9-11 (NKJV)

RECOGNIZING OVER EXPECTANT THINKING IN MYSELF AND OTHERS

People who are high in Over Expectant Thinking have a strong need to be right all the time. They may make their ideas or what they produce an extension of themselves, so they react in three ways when they are afraid, hurt, or offended:

1. They turn the negative feeling inward, producing self-critical or self-demanding comments.
2. They become self-righteous, overbearing, critical, or difficult.
3. They display Counterfeit Independence not Genuine Independence.

Does this sound all too familiar to you? In each of us there is a very special person, but the Over Expectant Thinking masks this intrinsic quality of who we are, leaving us unable to be a friend to our real self. The result is someone who is easily annoyed, who mimics his or her childhood history with critical and unfeeling comments, and who can be harsh and offensive. This isn't a Christ-like attitude.

UNDERSTANDING HIGH OVER EXPECTANT THINKING

If you are high in Over Expectant Thinking, recognize that being demanding, argumentative, and manipulative is not being assertive; rather, it's simply a struggle to find the real you. Who you are! It's not your negative attitude.

People with low scores in their Over Expectant Thoughts tend to be more cooperative and easier to please; they are more even-tempered and are not as easily provoked to anger. They have a much clearer picture of who they are and are more secure. People who are low in Over Expectant Thinking tend to be humble and will admit errors. They don't have to be right in order to feel okay about themselves. These people feel more secure with themselves and their own feelings and thoughts. They allow other people to be responsible for their own feelings and thoughts and they allow other people to be responsible without manipulation or control. They often do not like to be around people who are judgmental and critical. They see it as a waste of time and a source of drama. If you are low in Over Expectant Thinking you may find yourself to be Decisive and have a good sense of confidence. Your expectations may be realistic, and you tend not to be judgmental. You also may display Genuine Independence with real internal confidence.

INWARDLY OVER EXPECTANT

Sometimes Over Expectant Thinking is turned inward. Over expectancy and self- critical thinking can cause a person to "beat-up" on him- or herself, rather than creating difficulty for others. This inward Over Expectant Thinking is sometimes found in people who are shy. Think how you may be overly critical of what you do or say toward yourself.

This isn't to say that people who have a high Over Expectant Thinking style are bad people; in fact, most of these individuals are very critical of themselves when they don't meet their own expectations. This chapter is to help you to have a deeper understanding of the common problem Over Expectant Thinking creates. Even if you or your family don't have this thinking behavior, chances are good that you will encounter someone in your path of life that has this as a primary part of his or her personality. Since this is a good possibility, it is better to be prepared in how to deal with this person than to just fall prey to his or her demands. You may not be able to change this individual, but you can change how you deal with him or her. So, take charge with new equipping thinking tools.

If high levels of Over Expectant Thinking are your primary attitude, don't panic. There is good news, a new way to have control—self-control—and prevent alienating those around you. The payoff is closer, deeper, effective, and more enriched relationships. Better this than ending up alone, old, angry, and not knowing why.

UNDERSTANDING MODERATE OVER EXPECTANT THINKING

Moderately Over Expectant Thinking people are good problem solvers because of their critical thinking process. But good problem solving and critical thinking are also found in Decisive Thinking. In other words, to be a critical thinker you do not need to be high in Over Expectant Thinking. High Over Expectant Thinking creates internal fear, anger, and demand that literally can take a physical toll on the individual's body. High Over Expectant Thinking people need to concentrate on more positive ways to achieve their goals, taking into consideration what is a realistic time frame. They need to analyze constructively. Productive energy and accomplishment do not mean use of destructive critical thinking.

How This Can Cause Stress

People who are high in Over Expectant Thinking (and express it outwardly) have to be right to feel okay about themselves. Because of this, they need to control most of what goes on around them in order to deal with their own internal fear of failure. One way they do this is to put demands and "overexpectations" upon themselves and others.

Their thoughts impose unrealistic expectations that often go beyond what is humanly possible at the moment. This type of intensity is felt by other employees and customers to the point where people may quit, causing retention issues or customer service problems.

High levels of Over Expectant Thinking should never be confused with confidence. The contrary is more the truth. Over Expectant Thinking is more of a cover up out of fear of being wrong or fear of failure. This is why high Over Expectant people argue or are disagreeable in order to be "right." The attitude is, "If I am right, then I am OK, if I am wrong, then I am not OK." A note of caution: Ask yourself if the Over Expectant Thinking is turned inward toward yourself or outward toward others. People with inwardly Over Expectant Thoughts usually just beat up on themselves and are more self-critical than they are critical of others. This causes a lot of internal stress. Usually, it is other types of thinking that softens the Over Expectant Thinking or turns it inward, such as high Compassion, Self-Doubting, Self-Defeat, or Hypersensitive. If you have Over Expectant Thinking, list all the ways you set expectations too high. Create positive affirmations to counter these negative expectations. People who are inwardly Over Expectant Thinkers may constantly self-criticize. They become annoyed when things go wrong and needlessly badger themselves about the mishap of being human.

These people even make unkind remarks to themselves, judging themselves without mercy. Are you kind, tolerant, loving, and accepting of the person who lives inside you? If we are cruel to ourselves, we may be creating 'self-punishment'. How can we accept ourselves if we don't feel others can accept us? Some people go so far as to push people away because they can't accept love. This is more likely to be true if a person also has high "Self-Defeating" Thinking. If you find yourself in a self-punishing mode, start now to do things for yourself that are positive and tell yourself you deserve good things.

Have you noticed that the amount of energy you spend having to control your inner feelings and actions may be so overwhelming that you seldom allow yourself to have free time to do the things that bring you pleasure? People with highly Over Expectant Thinking may see themselves as superior to others or have a haughty behavior or have a strong need to control people and situations around them. "Control? I have never thought of it like that," you might say. You may have thought "the only way" was your way, or "If people only knew what was good for them, they would do what I wanted them to do. After all, I am right, aren't I?" Check out the energy loss you create for yourself by having to "keep tabs" on everybody.

Sometimes Over Expectant Thinkers maintain their position of being right by shifting blame and responsibility to someone else or creating communication diversions. It is "safer" to feel in control. These people become short tempered when people do not meet even the slightest of their expectations. Such people may be "rigid" or "set in their ways." If people try to use this approach to life, conflict will result at the price of "lack of emotional connecting." Such a person often demands, rather than earns, respect from family and friends.

High Over Expectant Thinkers can often dispute other people's ideas. They believe that if they are right, they are "acceptable." A high Over Expectant Thinking person may become easily annoyed or respond with harsh and unfeeling comments if someone disagrees with him or her. This way, the person manipulates the environment and the people around him or her, in order to gain comfort and control his or her personal fears.

SO HOW DO WE LEARN THESE BEHAVIORS?

A person high in Over Expectant Thinking may have grown up in an environment where there was another Over Expectant person—generally a hypercritical parent or sibling. Can you think of anyone who may have criticized you? Someone who frowned upon your feelings, ideas and efforts? Someone who may have said, "You are stupid! What is wrong with you? Why can't you do any better?" When we grow and develop, we begin to hear these critical words and store them in our childhood history (subconscious).

People high in Over Expectant Thinking often internally criticize their own decisions and rarely allow themselves to have any fun or pleasure. They can be upset about their own shortcomings, not giving themselves a break for their own humanness. They may expect unrealistic "perfection" and, falling short of this goal, judge themselves without mercy.

They will justify their behavior by saying, "If I'm that demanding on myself then other people should demand just as much of themselves. I'm expecting just as much from them and their production as I'm expecting out of myself." This is often a "projection." The high Over Expectant person's own internal struggle can be blamed on others. These people may be blaming others for what they are not able to achieve themselves. Now this does not mean the Over Expectant person is a bad human being. Of course not! As a matter of fact, he or she has set out to do great things. But high Over Expectant Thinking is detracting from the individual's success in working with people. The real struggle for these people is not knowing who they really are, so they fight within themselves to be right in order to feel OK. (See Chapter 1.)

People with high Over Expectant Thinking have a struggle for inner independence; however, it creates Counterfeit Independence. Genuine Independence is high Decisive Thinking and Self-Assured Thinking. The key is, that when you understand Genuine Independence Thinking, it will help you accomplish what you really want to achieve—the best thinking and attitudes that will benefit yourself and others.

> *"My dear brothers and sisters, take note of this: Everyone should be quick to listen, slow to speak and slow to become angry, for a man's angry, because human anger does not produce the righteousness that God desires."*
>
> JAMES 1:19-20 (NIV)

OVER EXPECTANT THINKING PEOPLE CAN BE GOOD PROBLEM SOLVERS

Moderate Over Expectant Thinking people, if left alone, are very proficient and they are content to complete a project. They only have to measure up to their own standards and no one else's.

A person with high Over Expectant Thinking is often motivated by fear, with an inner sense of insecurity. It is quite natural to experience insecurity considering all that criticism one has heard as a child. So, fear of not being "in control" develops. This is why people high in Over Expectant Thinking always have to be right. To be wrong is to be less in control of their inner fears, so these inner fears are hold them down—that is scary!

High Over Expectant people become argumentative, very demanding, and even rude and bossy to maintain their secure feelings. This is also why high Over Expectant people are unyielding in will and opinion. Have you ever felt that you "needed" your ideas to be right and to be accepted by others in order to feel "okay"? If so, your inner belief might be, "to be right is to be accepted." Over Expectant people tend to place extra emphasis on their own faults in order to protect themselves. After all, if they criticize themselves, no one else can criticize them. The opposite of being in control is trusting yourself to take care of you in any situation.

The need to control is reduced as we trust ourselves to set boundaries and limits, although not in a demanding way. We can then be spontaneous, moving in and out of situations and choosing relationships that nurture us.

If people have high Over Expectant Thinking, they can be resentful of their own shortcomings, and will not give themselves a break for their own humanness. They expect unrealistic "perfection" and, falling short of this goal, judge themselves without mercy. They may also project these same feelings on others, including the driving need to be right even if they are wrong. This detracts from emotional intimacy and connecting with people.

To be a critical thinker you do not need to be prideful or haughty. This may be news to an Over Expectant individual. Over Expectant people need to concentrate on the positive aspects of life situations more. They need to constructively produce positive encouragements (high Decisive and Self-Assured Thinking), which is less likely to cause destruction to relationships.

> *"Folly is joy to him who is destitute of discernment,
> But a man of understanding walks uprightly."*
>
> PROVERBS 15:21 (NKJV)

The urge to control others is only surpassed by the grief it causes in oneself.

UNDERSTANDING OVER EXPECTANT THINKING IN RELATIONSHIPS

STORY OF JOE AND PATTY

Joe and Patty had been married for 12 years and had two boys still in elementary school. Joe worked as a maintenance manager at a large mall and Patty had a half-day job as a receptionist in the local dentist's office. Their marriage on the surface appeared to be happy and they enjoyed socializing with their friends and family. One evening, when they were visiting friends at a barbecue party in the neighborhood, Patty's friend Nancy noticed that Patty seemed tense and had been quiet all evening. When Nancy approached her about this in private, Patty brushed it off and just said that she and Joe had a disagreement earlier in the day. "Joe just doesn't get it!" she said, "He just won't cooperate with me on really important things sometimes." Nancy asked more questions and eventually established that Joe had again worked late the night before when he had promised to help Patty finish the painting of some new shelving in the boys' room. Nancy defended Joe, pointing out that his work was important and overtime could not always be avoided. "Oh please, don't tell me you don't get it either!" Patty retorted, "We planned to finish the room last night no matter what. It's about time he realized that his family comes first!" Again, Nancy tried to explain to Patty that sometimes she expected too much of Joe.

"Well, you're lucky," said Patty. "Your husband doesn't let you down the way Joe does. Besides, I know that I am right about this and I am not going to back down. He has to start realizing that I can't accept lack of cooperation in this marriage." Nancy shrugged and walked away at that point. She realized that it was pointless trying to argue with Patty and rather than spoil the evening, she ended the discussion.

Later in the evening, Patty told Joe it was time to head home as the boys were getting tired. Joe replied, "Oh, don't worry so much, Patty. It's not that late.

We're having fun. The boys don't look tired to me." "The boys have soccer tomorrow, in case you forgot. Besides I think it's time to get home anyway, we've outstayed our welcome," said Patty. This push-pull discussion went on for a few minutes, as Nancy and her husband observed the "battle of power" with some amusement. As usual, Patty eventually got angry and Joe agreed to leave, in case she caused unnecessary unpleasantness. When they got home and the boys were asleep, Joe sat down with Patty and said he really wanted to talk. "Now, what?" thought Patty with irritation, as she put things away and prepared for the next morning's activities.

Joe then shared with Patty his frustrations at her "bossing attitude" in their relationship and that he felt no matter what he did it was never good enough. He said he sometimes felt that she didn't value or appreciate him and only enjoyed it when he "towed the line" and didn't disagree with her. He said that he couldn't take it much more and that she was making his life miserable. As a result, he actually enjoyed going to work—there, people appreciated him and didn't mind if he didn't always agree with them or do things their way. He did a superb job and was well liked. He said he wanted the same environment in the home. Patty was stunned. She felt that she had always assumed the dominant role in the household because that was what she expected of herself and that Joe was too soft and not always that responsible, especially with the children. But she told Joe that she really didn't want to hurt him, that she loved him very much. Fortunately, Joe and Patty were able, over a period of weeks, to spend time talking regularly about their relationship and Joe helped Patty begin to "soften" her approach and not become so angry when things didn't go her way.

> "A hot-tempered person must pay the penalty; rescue them, and you will have to do it again."
>
> PROVERBS 19:19 (NIV)

Examining the Impact

People high in Over Expectant Thinking are motivated by fear and have an inner sense of insecurity. Their fear of not being in control keeps their deeper fear from surfacing.

People high in Over Expectant Thinking also tend to find and emphasize faults in other people. Doing this is a means of building themselves up. These individuals often do not like to take blame or responsibility and will shift it to someone else in order to be right. Friends and family do not feel "cared for" in this environment. They may be afraid and may "tiptoe" so as not to provoke a disagreement. They may lose the friendship and respect of their friends or family members due to their demanding attitude, and sadly, may not know how to change this. Others may not see it, but it can cause an even deeper feeling of inner inadequacy. This can cause resentment toward others when they are "wronged" or "offended." They may even feel like "getting back" at the particular person. Most of the time the other person did not intend to hurt or offend them.

It is important that highly Over Expectant Thinking people learn the difference between aggression and healthy assertion. This is a common source of confusion. Some jobs do require aggressiveness, but negative aggression for aggression's sake is often counterproductive to reaching long-term goals. Assertiveness (high Decisive Thinking) plus a positive forward-thinking process (high Compassion Thinking) creates greater long-term production. Negative aggression tends to alienate people and can cause turnover and low morale in companies.

Jesus Is Our Living Example

Jesus was a very Decisive and positive person, as well as God. Jesus didn't have a haughty or prideful attitude. In fact, He didn't like people who were haughty in nature. A haughty individual is filled with self-centered, Over Expectant pride. Jesus was very perceptive, and could smell prideful individuals, and He knew they used their haughty nature to fill their own pockets and their prideful egos.

Jesus modeled for us not be self-centered or prideful. He modeled being humble, kind, loving, and compassionate. Jesus didn't put people down unless they showed to be a haughty self-centered heart. This should be an example for all of us to be humbler, kind, loving, and compassionate, which is real strength of character. Also, Jesus had a meek nature, which is strength under control, completely yielded to God with a compliant spirit to God and His Plan. Jesus was also merciful. He overlooks the shortcomings of others, showing undeserved kindness. Jesus's affectionate mercy helps us to be more like Him (showing spiritual maturity) and full of grace. Mercy is a giving attitude. Jesus's mercy doesn't point the finger, it shows compassion in action. Mercy saves the face of others and doesn't show judgment but rather forgiveness. The mercy Jesus models shows kindness to others and picks up the person.

> *"But the fruit of the Spirit is love, joy, peace, forbearance, kindness, goodness, faithfulness, gentleness and self- control. Against such things there is no law."*
>
> GALATIANS 5:22-23 (NIV)

JESUS MODELED THESE QUALITIES

He was understanding and displayed realistic expectations. He would deal with others in a positive manner showing great forgiveness. Jesus is the perfect model of how we should treat others. These are just a few of His wonderful qualities we need to model in our lives.

> *"A proud and haughty man-"Scoffer" is his name;*
> *He acts with arrogant pride."*
>
> PROVERBS 21:24 (NKJV)

THE IMPACT OF OVER EXPECTANT THINKING IN INTERACTIONS WITH OTHERS

During the course of a normal week, analyze a situation in your interaction with somebody (at work, family, or socially) that demonstrated your unrealistic, Over Expectant Thinking. Here are a few questions you can ask yourself and record the essence of the interactions.

ASK YOURSELF:

Who did I have unrealistic expectations (thoughts) about today?

What was the situation or circumstance that triggered these thoughts? How was I judging the other person?

Did this way of thinking place me above the person where I was looking down on this person and judging him or her?

Did this make me feel superior to the other person?

How is this controlling, unrealistic expectation thinking impacting my relationships with people, family, coworkers, and friends?

What is the benefit of not being judgmental of others and being more Christ-like?

> *"Judge not, and you shall not be judged. Condemn not, and you shall not be condemned. Forgive, and you will be forgiven."*
>
> LUKE 6:37 (NKJV)

We are all sinners and yet we are all called to be more Christ-like in how we interact with others.

Christ is such a wonderful example for us to model using His loving characteristics as our benchmark to emulate. He didn't need to judge others because He focused on showing love and compassion for others. This is real strength of character, and the bonus is we are made in God's image so by growing in His grace and example we are evolving to our true character (in Christ's image).

STORY OF HARVEY

Harvey is a lawyer in a large legal firm. He has worked for the firm for five years and wanted to be a partner of the firm. Harvey's style was to control everybody and everything around him. The junior lawyers under him were petrified because Harvey's style was demanding and unyielding. He wouldn't teach these new lawyers; he only made critical comments regarding something that they didn't do. If he could find a fault, he would pick it apart and demean the other person to the point of emotional devastation.

This made Harvey feel superior and important. It was also his way of protecting his position in the firm. One of the senior partners who had a reputation of being fair took Harvey aside and asked him to go easier on the junior lawyers. He explained to Harvey, "These people are working very hard to advance in our organization and it's our responsibility to help teach and develop them, in a positive and productive way."

Harvey, thinking his style was "right," continued in his old critical ways. Although he wasn't as blatant about his criticism of others, he still continued to control those around him. When it came time to choose new partners in the firm, Harvey got passed over. This devastated him. He started blaming everybody else except himself. It was easier for him to put the blame elsewhere because he didn't have to take responsibility for making changes himself. "He's right, therefore, they're wrong." Of course, he continued in his old ways.

EXAMINING THE IMPACT

The person who has a high level of Over Expectant Thinking is the result of internal fear, anger, or over expectations. Due to internal stress and self-criticism, these people can become their own worst enemies, sometimes suffering from back pain, headaches, and ulcers. At times these individuals can be so short-tempered and critical of themselves that they will push outward and become short-tempered with others. People who have this kind of thinking tend to argue points to be right in order to feel okay about themselves. Because of this, they need to control most of what goes on around them. One way they do this is to put demands and expectations upon themselves and others. This can cause great stress. Their expectations often go beyond what is humanly possible at the moment. This type of intensity is felt by coworkers, family members, and friends, to the point where they back off from risk of close relationships.

> *"You, therefore, have no excuse, you who pass judgment on someone else, for at whatever point you judge another, you are condemning yourself, because you who pass judgment do the same things."*
>
> ROMANS 2:1 (NIV)

IMPACT IN THE MARKETPLACE

Let's think about how the person with high levels of Over Expectant Thinking interacts with friends, family, or coworkers. Over Expectant Thinking causes a person to be domineering or overbearing. People may describe such individuals as "bossy by nature or even pushy." People high in this thinking may force their point of view as a "matter of principle." Do you need to win an argument, or are you so highly opinionated that you will argue over insignificant details that don't really matter?

It's difficult for Over Expectant people to admit an error. Being wrong in their mind makes them feel they have less control. Therefore, they can become demanding, even rude. They also can have an unyielding will and opinion. They need to have their ideas agreed upon by others. "Need" is the word to be emphasized here, because they need other people to say that their ideas are right in order to feel personally "okay." So, they may make their ideas or tasks an extension of themselves. How many business or family decisions are made just because someone "needs to be right" to protect their ego, even if the decision really was wrong?

Individuals with high levels of Over Expectant Thinking justify their self-criticism. They can be seen waving that big stick saying, "If I am this hard on myself, other people should be this hard on themselves, too. Maybe they will get somewhere in life, also." These individuals are short tempered with other people and project onto other people how they criticize and expect too much of themselves. They create a no-win expectation cycle. When something is achieved, it is never quite good enough. The message they constantly hear is, "No matter what I do, I am not enough." On the upside, these individuals at moderate levels can be productive. Their critical thinking is an advantage in this arena.

You may be wondering whether people can maintain their productivity and have better relationships if they reduce their Over Expectant Thinking. The answer is

YES! Critical thinking and good problem solving are also found in Decisive and Self-Assured Thinking. In other words, to be a critical thinker you don't need to be argumentative to deal with negative individuals. In fact, you will discover that you will not only maintain your productivity, but your successes and relationships can greatly improve. You are making a "win-win" proposition here. By giving up internal fear and anger that literally takes a physical toll, with the Decisive and Self-Assured Thinking we get in exchange a tremendous increase in productivity, inner harmony, and health! Not a bad trade!

What do you think you would like to change if you were to have another chance at your Over Expectant interactions (i.e., in what ways could you have overcome being self-critical, Over Expectant, argumentative, or demanding)?

By being able to recognize and understand these Over Expectant behaviors, you will be able to approach your communications with others more effectively and help them to overcome their need for controlling others. How do you observe this driver in yourself or others?

YOUR PERSONAL DEVELOPMENT PLAN

Up to this point in this program, you have spent some time gaining a deeper understanding of people high in Over Expectant Thinking and examining the impact on attitude, productivity, and relationships in your world. Now you are ready to begin the process of overcoming the need to control and building more positive interactions with yourself and others.

SKILLS TO OVERCOME THE NEED TO CONTROL

Challenge yourself to settle issues in a positive compromise. A win-win approach doesn't make you wrong. You can choose to learn self-control and choose to respect other's ideas, so you won't be seen in a negative way by others. Don't be surprised if people ask you questions in terms of "other people's needs" to help you become aware. People may want to pose a helpful challenge. They may say, "Joe, I'd like for you to see if you can find out Tom and Mary's needs on XYZ project this week. Let me know on Friday, when we get together again, how we can respond to their needs." This type of homework can help get beyond self-centered thinking. Being less Over Expectant can open the channels of self-acceptance. This, in turn, creates attitudes and behaviors that tend to be more understanding of others. Read Chapter 5 and learn how to be more compassionate.

Your first positive action toward improved interactions with others is to apply the following exercises toward success in the coming weeks. As you apply each of the following exercises, monitor your progress by noting situations that occur during the coming weeks, in which you applied each exercise.

USE CRITICAL "EXPECTATION ENERGY" IN A POSITIVE WAY

For example, analyze situations at home or work. Look to the positive and constructive attitude, rather than the negative. Your critical thinking processes will serve you and others in a healthier interaction when you use your Decisive Thinking in a positive manner to get your point across. It is very important to admit and recognize Over Expectant Thinking (in high levels) as it gets in your way of having healthy relationships.

PRACTICE ASSERTIVENESS VS. AGGRESSION

We must understand that there is a difference between NEGATIVE aggression and assertion. This is a very common mistake. We might say, "I am just being assertive," when, in fact, we are showing aggression. Negative aggression is not appropriate at home or at work. Now you might say, "What about salespeople? They have to be aggressive. That's good, isn't it?" It's a good idea for salespeople to be very assertive, but aggression, as defined here, is a negative thinking process or a critical attitude toward others that can result in striking out emotionally at others. This week practice getting your point across calmly and listening to other's points of view.

STIFLE REJECTING OTHERS' IDEAS

When new ideas arise, withhold that urge to reject them. Think through the situation. Bite your lip and think before you react. Think to yourself, "This is not a personal threat. This is another's idea." Welcome it. Someone else's idea takes nothing away from you!

ASK YOURSELF THESE QUESTIONS: WHY DO I NEED CONTROL? WHY AM I AFRAID?

Do I need to control my environment for fear that I might be wrong, or that others might hurt me if I am vulnerable emotionally? If I am wrong, will I really be rejected? Maybe I resist sudden change because I am afraid of being out of control or I am afraid of being controlled by others? How did I feel controlled as a child? Do I really have to be right in order to have value and feel accepted? The truth is you have value, whether or not you are right. Realistically speaking, no one can be right 100 percent of the time. No one will see us as less valuable if we are wrong. Most people understand it is human to be wrong some of the time.

We must never become so reactive that we justify our own aggression by "getting it off our chest." That is not justification for aggression. All it does is leave a trail of victims behind. Picture yourself getting mowed down like Custer's last stand. I am sure Custer was not comfortable, nor were the people around him. Stop and think again before you react. Any negative response is not constructive if it hurts someone else. People are more attracted to a person who demonstrates self-control and a positive attitude.

> *"Do you know that the unrighteous will not inherit the kingdom of God? . . . but you were washed, but you were sanctified, but you were justified in the name of the Lord Jesus and by the Spirit of our God."*
>
> 1 CORINTHIANS 6:9-11 (NKJV)

> *"My dear brothers and sisters, take note of this: Everyone should be quick to listen, slow to speak and slow to become angry, because human anger does not produce the righteousness that God desires.*
>
> JAMES 1:19-20 (NIV)

> *"Love suffers long and is kind; love does not envy; love does not parade itself, is not puffed up; does not behave rudely, does not seek its own, is not provoked, thinks no evil; does not rejoice in iniquity, but rejoices in the truth."*
>
> 1 CORINTHIANS 13:4-6 (NKJV)

Learn who you are so you do not make your ideas and what you do an extension of yourself.

LOVE YOUR NEIGHBOR AS YOURSELF

Celebrate yourself! Choose not to create emotional injury by being self-critical. Keep your expectations realistic. You are only human. Remember this: "If I am not in the now, I am nowhere. I can only expect what actually can be produced right now." Ask yourself, "Can anyone else really do any more than that?" Give yourself pats on the back for finishing a task in a reasonable amount of time. Give yourself kind, loving talks, talks of positive encouragement, when something doesn't go the way you expect it to. Above all, accept yourself for being human. Celebrate your humanness! You may find that you've become your own best friend.

Kindness is an extension of how Christ was kind to us by dying for our sins. Use Christ as the model for your life and life becomes much better.

OVER EXPECTANT THINKING—TRANSFORMATIONAL THINKING STATEMENTS
TRUTHS TO SET YOUR THINKING FREE

Check all that apply to you:

_____ If I expect more from myself or others than can actually be produced right NOW, I set myself up for disappointment, anger, frustration, or resentment—Instead, have realistic expectations like Christ. Nobody is perfect.

_____ I choose to not make projects, ideas, or tasks an extension of myself.

_____ I choose to have "realistic expectations" of others and myself.

_____ I choose to listen to what others are saying and not think of a rebuttal to prove my point when communicating. Be Christ-like—listen, listen, listen.

_____ I am OK even if someone doesn't meet my expectations. Christ loves those with faults—with His unconditional love.

_____ I choose to recognize what others are capable of "at the moment."

_____ I choose to control my "prove it to me" attitude and see the good in others like Christ.

_____ I choose to disengage from negative conversations. Complaining gets me nowhere.

_____ I choose to point out the good in situations—to be Christ-like in all I do.

_____ I choose to have self-control over any negative thinking.

_____ I will avoid passing negative judgment and be a more positive person like Christ.

_____ I will select my words wisely before I speak.

_____ Who I am has to do with my intrinsic value that God gave me.

_____ I choose to stop beating up on myself when I don't meet my unrealistic expectations.

_____ I no longer have to use prideful self-centered thinking. I choose Christ-centered wisdom over pride.

_____ I need to think about what the person is saying, not my feedback. Listen like Christ.

_____ I choose to communicate with my Decisive and Expressive Thinking, not my Over Expectant Thinking

_____ I will focus on my God-given intrinsic value and gifts rather than my behaviors.

_____ I choose to live a more Christ-centered life with myself and others.

**Read your Transformational Thinking Statements
three to five times a day or as needed.**

> *"Before destruction the heart of a man is haughty,
> and before honor is humility."*
>
> PROVERBS 18:12 (NKJV)

"Most assuredly, I say to you, he who hears My word and believes in Him who sent Me has everlasting life, and shall not come into judgment, but has passed from death into life."

JOHN 5:24 (NKJV)

"The wisdom of the prudent is to understand his way, But the folly of fools is deceit."

PROVERBS 14:8 (NKJV)

NOTES

CHAPTER 9

CONTRARY THINKING

Do You Ever Feel Like People Are Telling You What to Do?

INTRODUCTION

We all have had the experience of listening to some of the great comics of the world. They throw their digs at presidents, political issues, and people in the media. They entertain us, and we enjoy it. Regarding this cynical humor, what drives it? Cynical humor is often created from a person's Contrary Thinking. This thinking, in moderation, can be very fun loving and quite enjoyable. An important point to recognize is that people with moderate Contrary Thinking can be fun loving with their kind of fun cynical comments—it's a way of getting attention. This is okay if it doesn't intentionally hurt others or go against common sense etiquette.

We need to recognize that looking for more points of view is good as long as it doesn't push others to a point of annoyance. These individuals can use their scrutinizing thinking process as a means of "guiding others to a productive solution" as being "a challenging game" to get others to think.

On the other hand, if a person uses Contrary Thinking to hurt or put someone down in a critical fashion, rejection and emotional pain are the result. Sadly, our society has taken on the Contrary approach. The result has been bickering disputes, long legal battles, and being stuck in critical blaming cycles only looking at the past causes of problems instead of looking to quick, win-win solutions.

I guess if I were to create an example, I would say that Contrary Thinking is like a steak knife. When used properly, it is very functional and useful. If it is not used in a positive fashion, then it can be deadly or cause great harm. When reading this section, some people may think it is rather harsh. Remember, these are facts about this one thinking style. Some other more productive thinking can balance a person's attitude caused by the high levels of Contrary Thinking, for example, Decisive and Self-Assured Thinking.

The important thing to remember is that the Contrary Thinking creates a Counterfeit Independence. It is not Genuine Independence. So, if we want Genuine Independence (Decisive and Self-Assured Thinking) we will have to let go of the Contrary Thinking long enough to adopt a new more positive way of thinking, creating a better attitude.

Contrary Thinking is often associated with the skeptics of the world. They can use their thinking skills by analyzing solutions to challenges and guiding others to logical solutions. This is a stronger leadership approach and a more effective way to help others move toward positive solutions.

> *"A fool's wrath is known at once, But a prudent man covers shame."*
>
> PROVERBS 12:16 (NKJV)

CONTRARY THINKING

DO YOU EVER FEEL LIKE PEOPLE ARE TELLING YOU WHAT TO DO?

You can better understand where you are right now. Please check all the areas that apply to you in the list that follows:

*People **HIGH** in Contrary Thinking . . .*

_____ Are cynical thinkers—tend to be grumblers
_____ Self-screen their work—are self-centered
_____ Practice Contrary Thinking—negative thinkers
_____ Make negative or oppositional comments
_____ Have suspicious or non-trusting thinking
_____ Are disagreeable—resistant
_____ Resent being told what to do
_____ Don't close communication loops
_____ Make oppositional remarks
_____ Enjoy cynical playful humor

Biblical Character Example:
THOMAS

Strength: The person self-screens his or her work.

Weakness: This person may be overly suspicious and non-trusting of others.

*People **LOW** in Contrary Thinking . . .*

_____ May be too trusting or accepting of others
_____ Displays positive focus on problem solving
_____ Is pleasant in discussions and applies a positive approach

> *"For whoever exalts himself will be humbled, and he who humbles himself will be exalted."*
>
> LUKE 14:11 (NKJV)

> *"The foolishness of a man twists his way, and his heart frets against the Lord."*
>
> PROVERBS 19:3 (NKJV)

He who complains and feels he is being told what to do may miss the true wisdom of life.

RECOGNIZING CONTRARY THINKING IN MYSELF AND OTHERS

An important point to recognize—People moderate in Contrary Thinking can be entertaining with their fun-loving cynical comments—it's a way of getting attention. This is okay if it doesn't hurt others or cross over emotional boundaries of others. It is important to recognize that looking for other points of view is good if it doesn't push others to a point of annoyance.

People high in Contrary Thinking may take opposite sides in discussions (if it is their primary thinking). This becomes very grueling in meetings or in their personal relationships. In a conversation with a person high in Contrary Thinking, no matter what you say, the individual's response may be "I disagree." (Please note: This person's intentions are not bad; he or she is scrutinizing the situation in order to "be correct" in his or her thinking process.) This comes across as being a complainer rather than initiating change in a productive take-action manner. These people can appear as having an opposing attitude or just resisting other people's suggestions. Sometimes they may even resort to derogatory comments to support their position (or just to get others to "think"). It's like an internal game for them that often is perceived by others as condescending. If you ask cynical people why they respond this way, they will say, "It's a way of having fun, or it's a good way to put people on the spot to make them back up what they are saying."

Have you ever experienced life this way? If you have, you may have Contrary Thinking as one aspect of your thinking. High levels of Contrary Thinking can be a very counterproductive way of thinking. These individuals tend to believe this is a productive way to get people to think. It is a kind of a prove-to-me, convince me, attitude. It's often their way of trying to find out what other people are thinking. All of this, of course, is to create some sort of control, to throw someone else off balance. The difficulty with this type of thinking is that it can foster resentment and frustration in others, which creates a major block to emotional intimacy. These individuals may use these tactics to control the conversation or the environment. This person is trying to establish a sense of power or trying to look smart. This resistance and opposing attitude are the "beginning stages" of growth toward independence, often seen in adolescence. However, this creates Counterfeit Independence, not Genuine Independence.

If people have high Contrary Thinking and it is a primary method of thought, it can be very destructive. It can lead to a disposition that is resistant, unpleasant, non-trusting, and derogatory. This can erode self-esteem and the ability to connect with others. People high in Contrary Thinking may feel resentment when faced with an unpleasant task. The focus is on the dissatisfaction, the negative thinking rather than getting the task done. As a result, people with this thinking process tend to be resistant toward what others ask, rather than to initiate change. This is counterproductive and leads to internal dissatisfaction with themselves or relationships with others.

UNDERSTANDING MODERATE CONTRARY THINKING

People who score moderate in Contrary Thinking can have good results in task productivity since they possess just enough questioning to be productive. If a person also has high levels of complementary thinking skills like Decisive, Expressive, and Compassion, and are low in Over Expectant Thinking, he or she may be more effective, and is open to greater relationships and emotional intimacy.

UNDERSTANDING LOW CONTRARY THINKING

A person who is low in Contrary Thinking doesn't worry about whether or not someone is telling him or her what to do. These people realize that people are simply giving suggestions or sharing their opinion. Low scores in Contrary Thinking also indicate a person who is trusting and doesn't hold grudges. These people are quite cooperative and usually do not make cynical remarks. They often do not want to be around people who are high Contrary Thinking because they may feel that listening to someone complain and/or who is negative is a waste of time to be around. People who are low in Contrary Thinking understand that solving a problem is much more productive than complaining about it. They are more solution focused.

If you have low scores in Contrary Thinking you probably see the good and optimistic aspects of life, rather than cynical or negative aspects.

> *"These are grumblers, complainers, walking according to their own lusts; and they mouth great swelling words, flattering people to gain advantage."*
>
> JUDE 1:16 (NKJV)

UNDERSTANDING CONTRARY THINKING IN RELATIONSHIPS

STORY OF KEITH AND REBECCA

Keith and Rebecca had been dating for more than two years and were beginning to discuss marriage. Keith was a successful salesman in the insurance industry and Rebecca was an elementary school teacher. In the early days of their relationship, Rebecca was attracted to Keith's confidence and ability to hold intelligent conversations.

Keith, in turn, loved Rebecca's gentle spirit and her ability to endear all those with whom she interacted. She was genuinely caring and a good listener. He also always felt somehow "protective" of Rebecca and she responded positively to this attitude of his. When in the company of friends, Rebecca usually let Keith do the talking, but was sometimes uncomfortable at how he put people down when he didn't think well of them or disagreed with their ideas.

Keith had a tendency to pre-judge people and make derogatory comments about those who could not defend their opinions to him. But she didn't let it bother her too much, as he was so wonderful in other ways. One aspect of their relationship which Rebecca particularly enjoyed was Keith's quick humor and the ability to make her laugh. His impersonations of some of her favorite actors were so good that he would keep her entertained with his bantering when they were alone.

In the second year of their relationship, Rebecca was invited to become part of a task-focus group in the teachers' association, to investigate alternative methods of education for fourth graders. She was excited and told Keith all about it. She was crushed, however, when Keith said it was nothing more than just "overloading" the teachers' plates and that surely she realized that it would achieve nothing. The state would decide on what education methods would be used, so nothing they said or did would make any difference. Rebecca tried to get Keith to see it from her point of view, but he didn't listen and then passed a comment that it was probably just an excuse for her to "get away from him" considering the meetings were to be held in the evenings. Rebecca was really hurt but decided to go ahead with the meetings anyway and just not discuss the topic anymore. Keith, on the other hand, continued to make "barbed" comments whenever he could about the task force and many times accused Rebecca of "cheating" on him, as he had found out that two very nice single male teachers were in the same group. He took to driving Rebecca to the meetings and picking her up directly afterward.

One evening, the group decided that they wanted to go to a local coffee bar after the meeting and have cappuccinos. Rebecca said that she didn't think Keith would agree. One or two of her associates said to Rebecca that it was just ridiculous the way Keith "dogged" her around and that she should have her own freedom within the relationship. Rebecca defended Keith, but inside she knew they were right. Keith ended up going for coffee with the group, and on their way home Rebecca decided to speak to Keith about his attitude toward her. This ended up in a lengthy argument as Keith overreacted and said it just went to "prove" that he was right all along—the meetings with a group like that were just not good for her. Rebecca stood her ground. She also pointed out to Keith how his continual "belittling" of others and insistence to be right irritated her. She explained it was hard to continue loving somebody who could not be more caring and understanding toward others. She had grown tired of him being negative, cynical, and judgmental toward situations and people jumping to conclusions—often the wrong ones. By the end of her "outburst," Rebecca was in tears and felt so sad about having let out all her pent-up frustration and anger. They agreed to "cool off" for a couple of days. Unfortunately, that turned into weeks—Rebecca found a sense of relief not having Keith around and learned to like it. Keith to this day will tell you that Rebecca caused their breakup because she "got involved" with that group.

> *"Who is wise and understanding among you? Let him show it by his good life, by deeds done in the humility that comes from wisdom."*
>
> JAMES 3:13 (NIV)

EXAMINING THE IMPACT

A Contrary Thinker has positive and negative outcomes. In moderation, it can be very good. Moderate levels can produce a fun-loving, kidding personality that may self-screen or evaluate one's work. An example would be a good executive secretary who "covers the bases" for the company president.

The difficulty starts with high levels of Contrary Thinking, and these individuals don't like being told what to do, even when they are <u>asked in a kind way</u>. Similar to a rebellious adolescent, they will sometimes do the opposite of what they are asked as a way of proving their independence. However, this is Counterfeit Independence. Someone who has very high levels of Contrary Thinking can be very skeptical, annoying, and stressful to coworkers, family, and friends. This causes distance and prevents closeness. More time may be spent disagreeing about ideas rather than creating solutions. Flippant and contrary remarks may even be perceived by others as negative put-downs. Ask yourself—Are you getting your needs met by pushing others away with negativity and complaints?

> *"For a good tree does not bear bad fruit, nor does a bad tree bear good fruit. For every tree is known by its own fruit. For men do not gather figs from thorns, nor do they gather grapes from a bramble bush. A good man out of the food treasure of his heart brings forth good; and an evil man out of the evil treasure of his heart brings forth evil. For out of the abundance of the heart his mouth speaks."*
>
> LUKE 6:43-45 (NKJV)

By taking charge of Contrary Thinking and reactions such as complaining, making cynical remarks, or having an oppositional approach to communication, you can begin to achieve better, compassionate, thoughtful connections. The barrier of overprotection is lifted, which allows others to experience your Christ-like self. This new outlook will allow people to conquer overprotective, codependent patterns and sets the stage to feeling "cared for" by others. Exercise self-discipline by thinking before you react oppositionally to what others say.

Have you ever known anyone who complains to get attention or sympathy? There are other ways to get recognition and attention in a positive way so that it does not bring a subtle negativity to relationships. If taken to excess, Contrary Thinking can be disastrous in interaction with others. Observe someone who has a Contrary "devil's advocate" attitude. How does it affect others around him or her and the mood in group settings? Having someone play "devil's advocate" can be a grueling process. This person sets out to take a step forward, but is caught doing an opposing, repetitive dance. In reality, this person may be going nowhere. This type of activity fosters resentment and frustration in others, and slowly can wear away at a person's inner confidence.

If people have high Contrary Thinking as their primary approach to life it can be very caustic. It can lead to a disposition that is resistant, non-trusting, and derogatory. This strips away their ability to connect successfully with others.

Jesus Is Our Living Example

Jesus was a very straight shooter when He talked to people. He didn't have to prove He was smart by taking on a Contrary attitude. In fact, I think He saw right through people who had this approach. He also understood their struggle in their fight for genuine inner independence. He also knew that individuals with a Contrary nature were not as open-minded as they should be to learn the message of freedom and hope He was bringing into the world. Why? Because they are so self-absorbed, they don't have ears to hear or eyes to see. This is so sad, that doubting Thomas couldn't believe unless it was proven to him. Wow, what a sad way to think in life.

Jesus is a perfect example of being an open-minded, forward-thinking person who showed us to be open and humble to learn from Him and others. The good news! We can reach out to Him for encouragement and ask for His guidance in our lives.

Jesus Modeled These Qualities

He showed us how to be a positive thinker, trusting in Him and God's ways. He was not a grumbler, or self-centered, but a positive encourager, not negative, but open and thoughtful of others. Jesus teaches us to have self-control and not be resistant. Jesus shows us how to be trusting of God His Father, and to love and be of service to others. He was a great communicator and had playful humor. Let's use Jesus as our model and not have a contrary, oppositional, doubting Thomas attitude.

> "Whoever hides hatred has lying lips, and whoever spreads slander is a fool."
>
> Proverbs 10:18 (NKJV)

> "... He will teach us His ways, and we shall walk in His paths."
>
> Isaiah 2:3 (NKJV)

THE IMPACT OF CONTRARY THINKING IN INTERACTIONS WITH OTHERS

During the course of a normal week, analyze a situation in your interaction with somebody (at work, family, or socially) that demonstrated your Contrary Thinking. Here are a few questions you can ask yourself and record the essence of the interactions.

Ask Yourself:

Who did I have Contrary Thoughts about today?

What was the situation or circumstances that triggered these thoughts? How have I been contrary, negative, or disagreeable with others this week?

Did my Contrary "prove it to me" attitude make me look like the smartest person, yet negatively impact how others were feeling in my communications with them?

Did this make me feel superior to them?

How are my Contrary negative comments impacting my relationships with people, family, coworkers, and friends?

What is the benefit of not being resistant or non-trusting of others and being more Christ-like?

> *"The LORD lifts up the humble; He casts the wicked down to the ground."*
>
> Psalms 147:6 (NKJV)

Having a non-trusting attitude and being contrary in communicating with other people is not how Christ behaved. The goal is for us to be more Christ-like in how we interact and connect with others.

Jesus's loving examples should be our standard to model. He didn't need to look smart or have a "prove it to me" attitude toward others; rather, Jesus focused on showing love, grace, and compassion. If we are focused on developing real strength of character, then we need to focus on Jesus's example and evolve to our true character (in Christ's image).

> *"For the LORD takes pleasure in His people;*
> *He will beautify the humble with salvation."*
>
> Psalms 149:4 (nkjv)

Story of Ken

Ken was a new employee for a small manufacturing company. He got the job because his uncle was a friend of the owner. Ken reported directly to the production manager. On his first day on the job, he was given an employee manual and a job description. He was given a complete tour of the operation and was greeted enthusiastically by the owner.

As Ken settled into his new job, he was conscious of wanting to do well. The manager who he reported to was a very fast moving, fast talking individual. Ken began to get upset with the manager because he felt that he was being told what to do. Ken hated to be told what to do. So, his response to the manager was, "Sure, fine." But in his head, he was saying, "I'll do it when I darn well please."

Although Ken didn't blatantly not do his job, he slowed production down dramatically. This caused much turmoil in the production department. Other people's jobs were affected, and communication problems developed. Ken's Contrary behavior was his attempt at being "independent"; however, he never achieved this result.

Examining the Impact

When a high Contrary Thinking person doesn't want to do a particular task, he or she may complain about it. Other characteristics of a Contrary Thinking person are: fear of being taken advantage of, questioning people's motives, resistance to other ideas, and suspiciousness. Highly Contrary Thinking individuals feel people are "telling them what to do." They may also passively resist or decide not to accept another's suggestions as a way of trying to show their independence. People with a Contrary attitude can be very stubborn. Have you ever known a stubborn individual who holds on to an idea through thick or thin, grating on those around him or her without compromise?

IMPACT IN THE MARKETPLACE

In the work environment, a person may take the opposite side in a discussion just for fun, just for appearing as an independent thinker. Now you may be saying, "Wait a minute, people like this can be good performers." Having this type of thinking does not make a person bad. In fact, in some settings these individuals can be very funny. They can have a great sense of humor. Also, because they don't like to be told what to do, they may often self-screen their work. However, this is at moderate levels of Contrary Thinking.

A person with high Contrary Thinking is not letting his or her true potential shine through. This person may want to be extremely accurate just for the sake of feeling emotionally secure. Then, no one can question him or her. More can be achieved with this critical thinking process if it were used in a positive way (thinking before speaking). Understanding self-confidence is a direct result of our achievements. When a person is resisting suggestions or ideas and complaining about tasks, he or she is missing out on potential accomplishments. There is no new learning taking place because the doors to new knowledge and to new achievements have been closed. It is an unfortunate cycle; the Contrary person will often do the exact opposite of what he or she is asked to do.

This is a display of poor self-image and lack of security, plain and simple. "Nobody is going to tell me what to do" is the attitude. It is like an interested teacher telling a student, "I want you to get an 'A' on the next test." The negative and complaining, Contrary student passively resists and makes sure that he fails (even though he is very capable). Does this really bother the teacher? Who really wins here, and, more importantly, who really loses?

So, let's make sure that we are always winners. Let's lower our Contrary Thinking and increase our Decisive Thinking and Self-Assured Thinking (real independence).

> *"What causes fights and quarrels among you? Don't they come from your desires that battle within you?"*
>
> JAMES 4:1 (NIV)

The way of true Genuine Independence is Decisive Thinking and sanctified common sense.

He who complains and feels he is being told what to do may miss the true wisdom of life.

YOUR PERSONAL DEVELOPMENT PLAN

Up to this point, you have spent some time gaining a deeper understanding of Contrary Thinking and examining the impact this has in relationships and in your world of work. Now you are ready to begin the process of developing Genuine Independence as you reduce your Contrary behaviors in interactions with others.

SKILLS TO BECOME LESS CONTRARY AND DEVELOP GENUINE INDEPENDENCE

Your first positive action toward reduced Contrary Thinking is to apply the following exercises toward success in the coming weeks. As you apply each of the following exercises, monitor your progress by noting situations which occur during the coming weeks.

STAY OPEN TO OTHERS' IDEAS AND THOUGHTS

Before taking an opposite point of view, disagreeing or complaining, stop and ask yourself: "What can I gain in a positive way here? Yes, someone else has come up with a different idea. What can I learn from it? I am going to stay open." **This week, use your Decisive Thinking to lead others down a positive path to a positive conclusion.**

DISENGAGE FROM NEGATIVE CONVERSATIONS

Refuse to participate when people around you are being critical—having a complaining session. All too often we play "follow the leader" and simply join in the complaining game. Choose not to participate. Choose to change the subject. Here is an opportunity to develop an optimistic and cheerful outlook that can win out over negativism. **How can you use this in meetings at work this week or with family members?**

LOOK FOR THE GOOD IN OTHERS

By disliking other people, we dislike ourselves. So, in turn, we become disliked by others. Let's accept other people as well as we accept ourselves. Everyone has something good to offer.

Another wonderful behavior to develop is complimenting people in public, as well as in private. Let's be eager to express appreciation as well as praise. Rather than starting to take a Contrary point of view, start looking for ways to show appreciation for others' ideas and suggestions. It is hard to find time to complain if we are busy saying words of praise.

Plan on giving one person a day a "real compliment." Note this person's response. Do this for the next three weeks.

PRACTICE DIPLOMATIC DISAGREEMENT—POSITIVE LEAD-IN STATEMENTS

Having found some substitutes, let's now explore the direct attack. Let's use a positive lead-in statement or an introductory remark when we tell a person something that he or she may not want to hear. Here are some examples of lead-in statements. "I hesitate to tell you this, for fear you might get your feelings hurt, however," then finish your sentence. Another lead-in might be stated by saying, "I would like to clarify something." This gives the person a moment to prepare, to brace him- or herself. This is truly a safer way to make a comment without appearing too negative. You are still able to get the point of criticism across, but it is perceived in a complimentary, tactful, and diplomatic light. But, remember, even though we have discovered the way of the diplomat, we must still resist the urge to criticize. So, continue to praise the positive and take note of the results. This week use positive lead-in statements rather than disagreeing.

> *"But to Israel he says: 'All day long I have stretched out My hands to a disobedient and contrary people.. . . .'"*
>
> ROMANS 10:21 (NKJV)

AVOID BEING JUDGMENTAL

Do not judge hastily. When we judge others, we tend to judge ourselves. When we dislike ourselves, we feel bad and complain. A vicious cycle! So, rather than judging, search for the good in others and use your judgment to bestow a positive compliment. How can you compliment others on their idea—lead them to a more positive solution?

> "Then he called the crowd to him along with his disciples and said: 'Whoever wants to be my disciple must deny themselves and take up their cross and follow me. For whoever wants to save their life will lose it, but whoever loses their life for me and for the gospel will save it.'"
>
> MARK 8:34-35 (NIV)

> "But the fruit of the spirit is love, joy, peace, longsuffering, kindness, goodness, faithfulness, gentleness, self-control. Against such there is no law."
>
> GALATIANS 5:22-23 (NKJV)

Contrary Thinking–Transformational Thinking Statement Truths to Set You Free

Check all that apply to you:

_____I will recognize true Genuine Independence comes from having inner Decisive Thinking and Self-Assurance—True Genuine Independence is in Christ-like qualities.

_____I choose Genuine Independence and not behaving with false pride.

_____I will recognize when I'm being negative and with Christ's help correct this immediately.

_____I will be seen as a positive person. Christ was not a complainer.

_____I will question others with my Decisive Thinking (asking for positive solutions or steps), never in a condescending manner.

_____I choose to trust more in Christ and ask for His guidance daily.

_____I choose to risk being more loving, like Christ loves.

_____I am the kind of person who gets joy from being positive and loving.

_____I choose not to disagree for the sake of disagreeing, as this serves no purpose.

_____I will recognize that people aren't telling me what to do; they are simply suggesting their own ideas or making a suggestion . . . listen and respond as Christ would.

_____I choose to restrain my "prove it to me" prideful attitude.

_____I will offer viable solutions rather than being oppositional with others.

_____I may think with my Contrary Thoughts but respond verbally and deliver with my Decisive Thinking in a positive Christ-like manner.

_____I choose to disengage from negative conversations. Complaining gets me nowhere.

_____I choose to have an open mind and not take the opposite side just for the sake of creating frustration to look smart. (This is prideful behavior and not Christ-like.)

_____Complaining or just trying is not succeeding—Quit talking and be a doer, not a complainer.

_____You either do it or you don't, but do not try to get others to "prove everything to you" just to make yourself look smart. You may end up looking really stupid and negative.

_____Lead people through options to get to a solution by asking positive questions. It's a better choice.

_____Never make an assumption that people think you're stupid. Christ doesn't.

Read your Transformational Thinking Statements three to five times a day or as needed.

> *"Finally, brethren, whatever things are true, whatever things are noble, whatever things are just, whatever things are pure, whatever things are lovely, whatever things are of good report, if there is any virtue and if there is anything praiseworthy; meditate on these things."*
>
> PHILIPPIANS 4:8 (NKJV)

"The fear of man brings a snare,
But whoever trusts in the Lord shall be safe."

PROVERBS 29:25 (NKJV)

NOTES

CHAPTER 10

SELF-DEFEATING THINKING

Are You Hard on Yourself and Don't Accept Compliments?

INTRODUCTION

If you're like a lot of people you may have had feelings of failure or you may find fault with yourself. This can definitely lower your self-assurance and confidence. Right now, you can start learning the steps to build your inner strength and not let your inner gremlin control your life. It's time to quit putting yourself down. This chapter can develop your confidence by helping you to overcome Self-Defeating behaviors.

Self-Defeating Thinking takes away happiness and lowers your people skills, power, and self-esteem. Many years were spent developing the simple steps that help people to overcome their feelings of failure and self-put downs.

Remember to use the Transformational Thinking Statements at the end of this chapter. These exercises, when used on a daily basis, can give you the tools to overcome your Self-Defeating behaviors and to achieve more confidence. Your self-motivation will really make the difference. Your goal is to practice daily, or even hourly, the exercises to create new beliefs and attitudes as part of your life.

Don't let Self-Defeating Thinking ruin your life. Decide to conquer it now. Working through this chapter is a step in the right direction to developing your inner confidence.

> *"Have I not commanded you? Be strong and of good courage; do not be afraid, nor be dismayed, for the LORD your God is with you wherever you go."*
>
> JOSHUA 1:9 (NKJV)

> *"Be strong and of good courage, do not fear nor be afraid of them; for the LORD your God, He is the One who goes with you. He will not leave you nor forsake you."*
>
> DEUTERONOMY 31:6 (NKJV)

SELF-DEFEATING THINKING

ARE YOU HARD ON YOURSELF AND DON'T ACCEPT COMPLIMENTS?

You can better understand where you are right now. Please check all the areas that apply to you in the list that follows:

People **HIGH** *in Self-Defeating Thinking . . .*   ***Biblical Character Example:***
MATTHEW

_____ Have a giving up attitude
_____ Find it hard to accept compliments
_____ Look for the easy way out—have little self-confidence
_____ Play a victim role—find fault with themselves
_____ Experience a feeling of being overwhelmed
_____ Avoid risks—put self-down
_____ Are self-centered in their thinking

Strength: Highly aware and conscious of people and surroundings

Weakness: May avoid situations and experience feeling of failure

People **LOW** *in Self-Defeating Thinking . . .*

_____ Are likely to be more confident—enjoy taking risks
_____ Can accept compliments
_____ Are less likely to defeat themselves
_____ Look for things to accomplish

> *"For I say, through the grace given to me, to everyone who is among you, not to think of himself more highly than he ought to think, but to think soberly, as God has dealt to each one a measure of faith."*
>
> Romans 12:3 (NKJV)

> *"I can do all things through Christ who strengthens me."*
>
> Philippians 4:13 (NKJV)

RECOGNIZING THE SELF-DEFEATING THINKING IN MYSELF AND OTHERS

We can all think of someone who externally appears to have it all—intelligence, as well as common sense, aptitude in a chosen career, financial success, physical attractiveness, and a supportive circle of family and friends. It is often difficult not to envy someone so abundantly blessed. Yet, as we get to know this individual better, we often discover that this combination of good fortune doesn't provide real happiness. A "fortunate" individual may even be depressed. Why? He does not internally accept himself. Perhaps we can think of movie stars, family, or next-door neighbors with Self-Defeating Thinking? Or perhaps it applies to us. We can see how frustrating it is when we observe someone who appears to have it all and yet discounts himself. Have you ever felt this way?

UNDERSTANDING HIGH SELF-DEFEATING THINKING

People who have a high level of Self-Defeating Thinking operate from an inner struggle. This can be a very destructive pattern because it takes away a person's confidence. As people grow up, they gain a sense of confidence by taking on activities and proving that they can do them. To do this, these people had to go beyond the initial fear of failure. People can't just swing at a baseball once, and then give up because they missed and expect to feel confident about their ability to hit the ball.

People with high levels of Self-Defeating Thinking will often respond to outside experiences this way. They'll try something once and, unless they do it right the first time, they give up or find an excuse for not trying it again.

People with high levels of Self-Defeat play life safe. This causes them to be very non-assertive and they avoid taking risks because they are afraid of making mistakes.

People high in Self-Defeating Thinking often go around feeling tense and anxious, afraid of new ideas and experiences that may place them in a position of having to face a new challenge. This lack of confidence in themselves makes it hard to relate to others. Their lack of self-confidence is based on the fact that they have never really risked enough. They tend to accept situations as they are, rather than pursuing new challenges. They'll try something once and, unless they do it right the first time, they give up or find an excuse for not trying it again. People with high levels of Self-Defeating Thinking play life safe. This causes them to be very passive and they avoid taking risks because they are afraid of looking foolish or not succeeding.

People with high levels of Self-Defeating Thinking often avoid people or situations that could cause discomfort. This is a form of denial. What they do not realize is that facing a new situation will give them the self-assurance they need. If they pursued that situation and proved to themselves that they can do it, they would then gain confidence. The only way to feel confident and to become successful at any activity is to work at it until you conquer it. Then we feel more comfortable with the activity—like learning to ride a bike.

People with high levels of Self-Defeating Thinking find fault with themselves. The fault they see is that they are not like other people. This is a very common behavior among "'shy" individuals. They are afraid to try because they are afraid of not being perfect. These people often overprotect themselves by not taking on new challenges for fear of being less than perfect. (Therefore, there is little feeling of self-acceptance.)

A person high in Self-Defeating Thinking struggles with a pervasive sense of underachievement, wishing he or she had done more. Another characteristic shared by these people is the tendency to choose their words with the audience's reaction in mind. Thus, rather than just stating what is in their hearts, they will choose statements so carefully that they compromise themselves, telling people what they think they want to hear.

People with high levels of Self-Defeating Thinking are afraid of new approaches; they see only the potential for failure. These individuals need to identify this thinking clearly and make efforts to overcome this internal fear. People high in Self-Defeating Thinking must learn to challenge themselves, to take on new tasks (or seemingly difficult tasks) to prove to themselves that the tasks are not unachievable.

How This Causes Stress

People with high levels of Self-Defeating Thinking can be so afraid of risk that they may not approach people. An example would be people who need to get a job but put it off until they exhaust their reserved savings. Another example is a person who procrastinates after the first try at solving a problem. So, the problem gets bigger.

Some people feel they are defeating themselves. No matter how much they produce, they still feel they have failed or are not good enough. These individuals have narrow interests or play it safe in their interests. People who are high in Self-Defeating Thinking avoid situations that are new and risky, which have the potential for discomfort. Self-Defeating Thinking is a block against internal confidence. People who are constantly playing it safe, pushing away compliments, and telling themselves they are not good enough are robbing themselves of confidence. As children they may have been overprotected by parents, ignored, or heavily criticized. As a result, they may have developed Self-Defeating Thinking.

> *"Therefore my anxious thoughts make me answer, Because of the turmoil within me."*
>
> Job 20:2 (NKJV)

WHAT PEOPLE WHO CONQUER SELF-DEFEATING THINKING KNOW

One of the key characteristics of people with low Self-Defeating Thinking is that they are more willing to take risks. They find themselves feeling comfortable with taking on new challenges. Low Self-Defeating Thinking levels may also correlate with being a good decision maker. These people may also be a lot more confident in themselves as a result of knowing that they can take on new challenges and develop new skills.

People low in Self-Defeat don't look for the easy way out but find challenges to be interesting and exciting. They don't find themselves to be self-centered but look for fun experiences in life. These people are often quite objective in their approach and do not easily give up. They choose not to be overwhelmed but are challenged by life's circumstances. They ignore fear and take on challenges. This creates a sense of self-assurance and self-confidence because they do not defeat themselves before they try.

What if we all waited to feel safe before we took the risk of riding a bike for the first time? Most of us likely would never have learned to ride the bike.

> ***Never pick yourself apart for minor behavior problems or perceived failure.***

UNDERSTANDING SELF-DEFEATING THINKING IN RELATIONSHIPS

STORY OF TODD

Todd, a twenty-seven-year-old assistant manager of a hotel, has been frustrated in his career and has been in several unsuccessful jobs. Todd expressed his frustration to his friend at work, and stated that he wanted to change careers; however, the thought of making a move overwhelmed him. When he would get to the point of taking a risk, he found himself holding back. This would frustrate him, and he would get upset at himself.

When Todd's friend asked him what overwhelmed him about changing jobs, Todd talked about being afraid that he wouldn't find a job that he liked. So, rather than risking his security, Todd just didn't go out and apply for another job at all. It became very clear to his friend that Todd had a fear of risk. Todd was experiencing an inner struggle and it was affecting his self-assurance and confidence.

Over the next several months his friend worked with Todd on how he could increase his confidence while overcoming his Self-Defeating behavior. The friend explained to Todd that the only way he was going to have more confidence was to take the necessary risks and face his fear of failure. His friend explained that Todd was already failing by not going after what he wanted. Todd then realized that the worst thing that would happen is that he'd have to try again until he succeeded. If Plan A didn't work, he'd have to move on to Plan B, until he met his goal.

This new understanding helped Todd to develop a new career path. Within a matter of three weeks he began interviewing for new jobs and was hired for a job that he really enjoyed.

EXAMINING THE IMPACTS

Some people blame themselves for everything that goes wrong, even if they are not responsible for it. This causes a lot of inner turmoil and can eventually result in passive/aggressive behavior. People high in Self-Defeating Thinking must learn to challenge themselves, to take on new challenges (or seemingly difficult tasks) in order to prove to themselves that the tasks are achievable.

People you love can be confronted and lovingly encouraged to take on reasonable challenges. As they meet these challenges, they can then experience feeling more confident. If you know individuals with Self-Defeating Thinking you can give them verbal encouragement when they have completed a task, and don't allow them to discount the compliment. This will reinforce to them that they "can do it" and that somebody cares enough to challenge them to prove to themselves that they can achieve their goals.

Perhaps you have discounted a compliment given to you? For example: "Oh, it's really not that good." "Oh, it's just an old dress." "You know, I'm really not up to par." Have you found within yourself an inner struggle between positive and negative feelings? Have inner, negative feelings usually won, leaving you feeling defeated? If any of this sounds all too familiar to you, and has affected your relationships, self- defeat may be having a negative effect in your life.

> "... being confident of this very thing, that He who has begun a good work in you will complete it until the day of Jesus Christ...."
>
> PHILIPPIANS 1:6 (NKJV)

THE IMPACT OF SELF-DEFEATING THINKING ON INTERACTIONS WITH OTHERS

During the course of a week, analyze a situation in your interaction with somebody (at work, family, or socially) that demonstrated your Self-Defeating Thinking.

Here are a few questions you can ask yourself and record the essence of the interactions.

ASK YOURSELF:

When did I have Self-Defeating Thinking today?

What was the situation or circumstances that triggered these thoughts?

How was I looking for the easy way out or passing negative judgment on myself? Did my Self-Defeating, giving up attitude prevent me from connecting with others? Did this make me feel like less of a person around others?

How is Self-Defeating Thinking impacting my relationships with people, family, coworkers, and friends?

What is the benefit of taking reasonable risks and being fearless and more Christ-like?

> *"But immediately Jesus spoke to them, saying, 'Be of good cheer! It is I; do not be afraid.'"*
>
> MATT 14:27 (NKJV)

We all have fears that hold us back in some form, yet we are all called to be fearless and more Christ-like in how we interact with others.

In Scripture we are told "do not be afraid." We are not made to be victims. Jesus was a risk taker and was extremely confident. He didn't just try; He was a doer. This is real strength of character, and we are made in God's image so we also can take moderate risks and grow in His grace.

STORY OF MARYANN

MaryAnn was a junior in college. She was a nursing major. Her grades were fairly good: B's and C's. She had difficulty in raising her grades. It wasn't because she wasn't smart enough. She had an IQ of 147.

MaryAnn had another good quality—she was exceptionally beautiful. Many of her friends would give her compliments about how nice she looked, and MaryAnn's response would always be the same: discount the compliment. Mary never felt comfortable accepting a compliment; in fact, she was very self-critical. Her friends would even say to her, "MaryAnn, quit being hard on yourself."

MaryAnn had a part-time job on weekends as a secretary. When she started this job, she was required to learn a new computer program. MaryAnn felt overwhelmed and felt like quitting.

MaryAnn was high in Self-Defeating Thinking. This caused her to avoid situations and have feelings of failure, find fault with herself, and avoid risks. Even though she had a high IQ and was gorgeous in appearance, internally she felt like she didn't deserve much out of life. In fact, there were times when she felt like just giving up, even to the point of committing suicide. MaryAnn ended up just settling for a secretarial position after college because she was afraid of taking the risk for a new job. This baffled her family and friends because everyone who knew her felt she sold herself short of her real potential.

What would you say to MaryAnn? How can she be helped?

> "... He will teach us His ways, and we shall walk in His paths."
>
> ISAIAH 2:3 (NKJV)

> "As soon as Jesus heard the word that was spoken, He said to the ruler of the synagogue, 'Do not be afraid; only believe.'"
>
> MARK 5:36 (NKJV)

EXAMINING THE IMPACT

People with high levels of Self-Defeating Thinking have a feeling of constantly being unable to achieve their goals in life. They continually undervalue their own accomplishments no matter how big or how small these might be. They have difficulty accepting and receiving a compliment and tend to discount things that people say that could build their self-confidence.

People with high levels of Self-Defeating Thinking feel overwhelmed easily by new changes and may hold back and make excuses rather than face changes. This can impact a person's ability to make decisions, solve problems, and move in new directions when positive change is necessary. People who are high in Self-Defeating Thinking may never achieve their full potential and always perform at a less than realistic level as a result.

Jesus Is Our Living Example

Jesus was a very Self-Assured person who knew how to take risks. Jesus is a perfect example of being a strong person and doing this in a positive way. Jesus was encouraging of others to not be afraid, and to trust in Him.

We also can be reassured that Jesus's nature is understanding how we feel and struggle in our lives. We can reach out to Him, trust in Him taking on His encouragement, and ask for His guidance in our lives. This gives us permission to take calculated risks to gain confidence and be more Christ-like.

Jesus Modeled These Qualities

He showed us how to be of good courage and have confidence because we are made in God's image. Jesus showed us how to be courageous and take risks by relying on and trusting God; we are not alone when we are with Him. He also modeled for us how we can be less likely to defeat ourselves, as well as look for things to accomplish in God's will.

Jesus is the perfect model of how we should live not in fear, but in hope, as well as how to treat others. These are just a few of His wonderful qualities we need to model in our life.

How do you observe Self-Defeating Thinking in yourself or others?

In what situations have you seen or been involved with something where a high level of Self-Defeating Thinking was evident?

List some ways in which you can either help yourself or others overcome the Self-Defeating Thinking.

What is the cost of high levels of Self-Defeating Thinking in personal relationships?

YOUR PERSONAL DEVELOPMENT PLAN

Up to this point in this chapter, you have spent some time gaining a deeper understanding of Self-Defeating Thinking and examining the impact, in relationships. Now you are ready to begin the process of overcoming Self-Defeating Thinking behaviors and building new confidence.

SKILLS TO OVERCOME SELF-DEFEATING BEHAVIOR AND BUILD SELF-CONFIDENCE

What to Consider

Go easy and be very encouraging to yourself when you tackle Self-Defeating Thinking. You could take positive suggestions and not use them as personal character flaws.

- Always be self-encouraging.
- Take a small step at a time, so risks aren't so overwhelming. You don't need to swim the English Channel, just a lap in the pool will do. Try the second lap in the pool tomorrow. Remember: You didn't learn to be confident driving a car in one day.

Develop a "never give up" attitude. So, what if Plan A didn't work—no big deal. Go to Plan B. Go for your goals.

Your first positive action toward improved confidence is to apply the following exercises toward success in the coming weeks. As you apply each of the following exercises, monitor your progress by noting down situations that occur during the coming weeks.

Begin to Take Some Risks

Look at ways that you can expand your interests. People who only stick with comfortable, familiar ways can be dull and stifling, like a bird in a cage. The real freedom is outside of the cage. You may want to start playing a musical instrument like the guitar or piano or maybe make the first move in talking to people. Go on a new event or stretch your responsibilities at work. Use common sense. Calculate your risks. You will feel like you are growing. It is great to grow emotionally. Watch. People will be very supportive of you. For example, explain to your coworker or boss that you would like to try a little harder. Could they bear with a few mistakes? They will probably say, "Sure, we have been waiting for you to do it. I am glad you have decided to take action." Non-risk taking is a very strong inclination for the Self-Defeating person. Do you remember learning to ride a bicycle for the first time? Most of us lacked confidence. The wheels wobbled and we wondered whether or not we would fall and skin our knees. Yes, we lacked confidence; however, even though we may have skinned our knees, we got back on that bicycle and tried again and again. It was uncomfortable, but the more we tried, the more comfortable and the more confident we became.

What are two areas in which you can take a moderate risk to lower the Self-Defeating Thoughts?

SPEAK UP AND EXPRESS YOUR NEEDS

Don't wait for people to read your mind. The "expectant mind reading game" must be overcome. The worst that will happen is that they will express their idea in return. Nobody can read your mind, so express your expectations and needs clearly. You have a greater chance in getting your needs met. This week speak up and express your needs?

LOOK AT AREAS IN YOUR LIFE YOU ARE AVOIDING

A way to improve confidence is to list the areas in your life you are avoiding. Is it really worth avoiding? Maybe you can achieve and overcome the troublesome areas, one by one. When you face what you have been avoiding, you will feel more confident and self-assured. Start slowly in the beginning and work your way up the confidence ladder. You will find that you can be more successful than you ever thought you could be.

This week find two situations in which you can conquer this fear.

FACE PROBLEMS

We must recognize that problems do not go away by themselves. Why not face them and get them over with? If you face them, at least you don't have them hovering in your mind. It is true that it can be scary; however, once you face and overcome your fears, they disappear. Why? Because the problems are resolved. As we resolve problems, we take charge of our lives. We feel good because we have overcome the obstacles rather than letting them defeat us.

What is one problem you are going to face and solve?

PINPOINT AREAS OF WHICH YOU ARE AFRAID

Ask yourself, "What is the real threat? Is it just a perceived threat?" We can devise a plan to overcome the things in our life that are perceived threats or fears. So, step-by-step, you can feel more competent. Beat your fears; never let them beat down the real self within you that is trying to emerge. What are two perceived threats that are not "real" threats?

Recognize That No One Is Perfect

No one can do anything perfect the first time. It is impossible. There is no such thing as perfection!! So, choose to take that first step without feeling you have to do it perfectly the first time or the second or third. Never stop until you have reached your goal. It is an effort, but that's reality. Nothing worthwhile is easy.

Pick two things and don't do them quite as perfectly as you would normally. This could save you time.

Learn to Accept Compliments

Stop yourself from discounting compliments. Stop. Take a deep breath and receive the compliment. Say thank you! Appreciate it and bathe yourself with kind words at that moment. Tell yourself that you deserve it and you need this confidence booster. *Never discount a compliment this week.*

Choose not to be afraid of life. See that life is worth living!

> *"Though an army may encamp against me, my heart shall not fear; Though war may rise against me, in this I will be confident."*
>
> Psalms 27:3 (NKJV)

Self-Defeating Thinking—Transformational Thinking Statements
Truths to Set Your Thinking Free

Check all that apply to you:

_____I choose to take charge of my fears, not have my fears take charge of me. The Lord is about love not fear.

_____I choose to live for TODAY. The past is gone forever, and I can't do anything to change it. I will do what I can now!

_____I will achieve what I can now, even if it's not perfect.

_____If Plan A doesn't work, I will go to Plan B, C, or D. I will achieve my goal.

_____I choose to never be defeated. I can do all things through Christ Jesus who strengthens me.

_____I will keep working toward my goal. I only fail when I quit.

_____I choose to be successful by having a never give up attitude in the Lord.

_____I will do the best I can. No one is perfect.

_____I choose not to be helpless. I may not know how to do a task, but I will learn.

_____I will accept compliments and choose not to discount compliments.

_____I choose to have positive thoughts all the time with a Christ-like attitude.

_____I will take more selected risks to learn new things. Christ overcomes my fears.

_____I choose self-assurance by learning from my small risk, realizing I can do most anything I put my mind to with Christ's help.

_____I choose to have a never give up attitude—I will have an "I will go do it now attitude."

_____I will keep working toward the goal; I fail only when I quit.

_____I will not let my fear of failure keep me from doing what I need to do.

_____I will be in control of my fears, and not let my fears control me trusting in Christ's guidance.

_____I will not be so hard on myself and look at the good I can accomplish with the Lord's help.

_____When I feel out of balance, I will read my transformational affirmations.

_____I can't change the past, but I can learn from it with Christ's help.

_____No longer do I say "Maybe" or "Try," but instead I say, "I choose to" and go after the goal.

_____I build confidence and trust in the Lord by giving my fears to Him.

_____I don't need to focus on ME but on trusting in the Lord in all things.

_____Practice my Who Am I? Exercise—DAILY.

_____Everything I attempt is a learning situation, not a potential failure.

_____Look at the 99 percent as correct and humbly <u>not focus</u> on the 1 percent of imperfection.

_____I choose to think positively and create forward momentum. I do not hesitate toward my goals—I can do all things in Christ.

**Read your Transformational Thinking Statements
three to five times a day or as needed.**

Wait on the LORD; Be of good courage, And He shall strengthen your heart; Wait, I say, on the LORD!"

Psalms 27:14 (nkjv)

"Because I feared the great multitude, And dreaded the contempt of families, So that I kept silence And did not go out of the door."

JOB 31:34 (NKJV)

NOTES

CHAPTER 11

HYPERSENSITIVE THINKING

Have You Ever Felt Overly Self-Conscious?

INTRODUCTION

A good number of people in our society get their feelings hurt easily or go through mini "panic attacks." This may happen when they worry about people staring at them, when they walk into a room, or when they have to give a speech. A person gets that flushed and anxious feeling when the adrenal gland kicks in. Some people may describe this as feeling easily embarrassed. This comes from Hypersensitive Thinking. This particular type of thinking also can be a cause of arguments in relationships when individuals take things personally, feel hurt, and then overreact.

Have you ever gone through a situation in your life where you took something personally only to be embarrassed by misinterpreting what the other person said? I think many of us have. This chapter has been designed specifically to help you overcome feeling Hypersensitive.

This chapter has helped thousands of people via a very concise, concentrated format giving you the effective steps to stop feeling Hypersensitive.

To overcome the Hypersensitive Thinking, you need to practice the exercises on a daily basis. Want to lower your stress? If so, this chapter is a step in the right direction to learn how to not overpersonalize what people say and stop worrying what people are thinking of you.

> *"Be anxious for nothing, but in everything by prayer and supplication, with thanksgiving, let your requests be made known to God; and all peace of God, which surpasses all understanding, will guard your hearts and minds through Christ Jesus."*
>
> PHILIPPIANS 4:6-7 (NKJV)

HYPERSENSITIVE THINKING

HAVE YOU EVER FELT OVERLY SELF-CONSCIOUS?

You can better understand where you are right now. Please check all the areas that apply to you in the list that follows:

*People **HIGH** in Hypersensitive Thinking . . .*

_____ Are very sensitive and overpersonalize situations
_____ Have a tendency to misinterpret what people say
_____ Take other people's problems personally
_____ Let emotions overrule sound judgment
_____ Are overly sensitive and are easily hurt
_____ Are easily embarrassed

Biblical Character Example: PETER

Strength: The person is very sensitive toward others.

Weakness: This person may overpersonalize situations and is easily hurt.

*People **LOW** in Hypersensitive Thinking . . .*

_____ Can be very objective
_____ Are not easily hurt
_____ Respond, rather than react, to situations
_____ Can be more confident

> *"Whoever has no rule over his own spirit is like a city broken down, without walls."*
>
> PROVERBS 25:28 (NKJV)

> "I sought the LORD, and He heard me, and delivered me from all my fears."
>
> Psalms 34:4 (NKJV)

RECOGNIZING HYPERSENSITIVE THINKING IN MYSELF AND OTHERS: LOW HYPERSENSITIVE

Somebody who is low in the Hypersensitive Thinking does not overpersonalize and is not easily offended. These individuals tend to be very objective. They are rational, so they respond rather than overreact. They let their sound judgment control their emotions and their feelings. They do not find themselves easily embarrassed and they certainly do not take other people's problems personally. People with a low Hypersensitive Thinking are clear decision makers. They may have grown up in an environment where people were very objective in their nature. People with low Hypersensitive Thinking often do not jump into other people's problems but have the ability to step back and objectively analyze without engaging in the emotional trauma that may be going on around them.

How It Causes Stress

Individuals who have high levels of Hypersensitive Thinking usually experience inner stress. In fact, the Hypersensitive Thinking is one of the biggest internal stress factors in our society today. These individuals are easily offended, even when no offense was intended.

Hypersensitive Thinking individuals have difficulty accepting criticism; they worry about other people's opinions and they feel people are analyzing or criticizing them. They feel stared at and are easily embarrassed. Hypersensitive people feel responsible for others' moods and problems, often taking on their problems personally.

When a Hypersensitive Thinking person walks into a room, he or she will have an anxiety rush and wonder, "What is wrong with me, why are people looking at me?" Hypersensitive Thinking individuals are usually overly sensitive. They tend to overpersonalize what other people say and, as a result, get their feelings hurt easily. They feel uneasy in new situations and are usually concerned with and affected by other people's moods. They may even feel responsible for other people's moods and problems.

Hypersensitive Thinking is subtle in that it is like a fire under a corked bottle. It is just a matter of time before the cork blows. When you add high levels of Over Expectant Thinking you may find a person who blows up for no apparent reason. This can cause major conflicts, as well as stress in relationships.

In the case of an overly sensitive person with a high level of Hypersensitive Thinking and high levels of Self-Defeating Thinking and/or Self-Doubting, this person will desperately want to please. However, the inner pressure may build to the point where the person may pout or just quit talking. Underneath, this individual is afraid to speak out for fear of being rejected emotionally if someone doesn't accept his or her opinions or ideas.

A Hypersensitive Thinking person should learn to control his or her internal, easily embarrassed feelings, for both emotional and physical health. Choosing "perceived reality" over "true reality" creates tension and anxiety. The body reacts as a stress/anxiety signal to let the person know that he or she has to work at overcoming this overly Hypersensitive Thinking and feeling.

WHAT TO CONSIDER

How can anyone establish close relationships on a consistent basis if he or she is feeling hurt, taking things personally, overreacting, or withdrawing as a result of being so Hypersensitive? If two people interacting have a high level of Hypersensitive Thinking, there is a dramatic increase in poor communication and lots of drama. I would liken the Hypersensitive Thinking to "fuel for the fire." When individuals are able to lower their Hypersensitive Thinking, it's like taking the fuel away. This can pave the way for more open communication and a good start toward stronger relationships.

We can begin by seeing that our loved ones and friends are not out to offend us or hurt us. If this is the case, then we need to tell the person that we deserve to be accepted for who we are, and not just what they expect from us. However, if you are high in the Hypersensitive Thinking you may be too afraid to positively confront others and consequently just settle for a relationship that is lacking in integrity.

If you are fortunate to have a positive supporting relationship and your tendency has been to take comments personally, then you can begin to focus outward to see that others may be overly sensitive just as you are. This outward focus will help get your mind off an inward, negative track. Look at people—they have their own problems. Focus on not making someone else's problem yours. Let other people have a bad day while you stay up. The only way we own someone else's problem is if we choose to "buy into it." Choose not to buy into someone else's problems.

When you are around people, say to yourself, "I choose to listen to the content of what others are saying and choose to keep it neutral. I choose not to read into others' tones of voice. I choose to let others have a bad day and I choose not to let their problems become mine." Say this to yourself each time you feel the "anxiety" rush, or you feel defensive.

Anxiety is a direct result of seeing reality differently than the way it really is.

UNDERSTANDING HYPERSENSITIVE THINKING IN RELATIONSHIPS

STORY OF SUSAN

Susan has worked as a telephone operator for about five years. She quickly learned how to handle customers in a positive way because she was well trained. One of the reasons Susan enjoys working as a telephone operator is because she is very sensitive and doesn't have to deal face to face with the public.

Susan has had a boyfriend for the past two years and, on occasion, she and her boyfriend would get into discussions and Susan would get her feelings hurt easily. Sometimes she would react by suppressing her emotions and other times she would react by blaming her boyfriend or rejecting him. Often, she would find herself becoming embarrassed because she would recognize that what she had taken personally wasn't meant that way at all. She had been "reading into" what her boyfriend had said. She usually had an anxiety reaction. One of her ways of coping with her Hypersensitive Thinking was to work in a job where she wouldn't have to have direct contact with customers.

Susan expressed to her girlfriend that her feelings were easily hurt and that she was extremely sensitive. Susan said, "Sometimes I just don't understand why I react the way I do. It seems that when I walk into a room and people look at me, I get frustrated and embarrassed. I'm always worried about what somebody is thinking, especially my boyfriend. I'm constantly asking him questions, wondering if I'm reacting the right way or saying the right things. It's very stressful for me."

Susan's anxiety level was very high because her level of Hypersensitive Thinking measured in the extreme levels. Susan told her girlfriend that she would misinterpret looks that people gave her or the tones of their voices and become extremely anxious.

Does this sound familiar to you? Do you want to stop being Hypersensitive like Susan?

EXAMINING THE IMPACT

High levels of Hypersensitive Thinking are developed in early childhood. A child will interpret the looks or tone of voice of a parent or older sibling. Maybe someone in your family was hypercritical, snapping at you abruptly or glaring at you. You may have learned to interpret a glaring look or an abrupt tone of voice as negative. Later on in life, the subconscious continues to deliver the same message whenever someone looks at you in an inquisitive manner. As adults, we may continue to jump to negative conclusions before truly understanding what is really being said.

We become emotionally vulnerable to what other people say, getting our feelings offended by a tone in someone's voice or a blank look that never was intended to hurt us. For our own emotional and physical health, we need to learn to overcome our Hypersensitive feelings. Stress, anxiety, and nervousness are not good for our health and well-being. They can take away our enjoyment of life. They are symptoms telling us that it's time to make some changes.

High levels of Hypersensitive Thinking are found in the majority of the population and are among the easiest thoughts to overcome. If you are overly Hypersensitive and have a self-centered approach to life, it is easy to recognize, because it causes a fear reaction. The body shoots out adrenaline, causing an anxiety rush and creating that flushed, "mini panic attack" feeling.

Individuals who are high in Hypersensitive Thinking usually misinterpret what other people say, and inevitably experience hurt feelings. The Hypersensitive Thinking person may jump to the wrong conclusions before truly understanding what is being said. This individual becomes emotionally vulnerable to what other people say. This typifies Hypersensitive people. Since they negatively interpret other people's reactions, their bodies respond accordingly. They may have sweaty palms, feel their face flush, or have a lump rise in their throat. This overreaction may seem inappropriate to other people and, when confronted, this creates very embarrassing situations. For no apparent reason, overly sensitive people may blurt out a remark that is totally "off base" because they may let their emotions overrule their sound judgment.

An overly Hypersensitive individual must recognize that he or she is not always the center of attention. Individuals high in Hypersensitive Thinking see the world as a hostile audience forever watching them. Their every move is scrutinized. True, a few individuals may preoccupy themselves this way, but the majority of people are too busy worrying about their own problems, or they may be Hypersensitive themselves.

Jesus Is Our Living Example

Jesus was very understanding and compassionate with people, because He was not Hypersensitive at all. He displayed a calm and controlled loving demeanor. This allowed other people to just be themselves without fear of Him overreacting, even when they were fearful, sinful, or just did dumb things.

Jesus, being calm and objective, could then pick-up on the feelings of others without them even saying anything. He understood what they were going through. He understood their struggles, because He was not fearful. Jesus was the most balanced person walking the face of the earth, so when others expected Him to overreact and he didn't, this shocked people. This allowed Jesus to not be manipulated by the political or religious powers of His day, which amazed people. What a powerful example for us to follow and model ourselves after. Let's live our life with objective thinking with Christ-like qualities.

We also can be reassured by Jesus's nature of understanding how we feel and struggle in our lives. We can reach out to him for encouragement and ask for His guidance in our lives.

Jesus Modeled These Qualities

He is very objective and is not easily hurt. Jesus modeled for us how to be a responder and not a reactor to situations, unless the situations were really out of line and out of his Father's will. He displayed a calm cool confidence that was very appealing to others, which made Him very magnetic when people were around Him. This shows us what great leadership and "right living" is all about. Jesus is the perfect model of how we should treat others. These are just a few of His wonderful qualities we need to model in our life.

> *"You dear children, are from God and have overcome them, because the one who is in you is greater than the one who is in the world."*
>
> 1 John 4:4 (niv)

THE IMPACT OF HYPERSENSITIVE THINKING IN INTERACTIONS WITH OTHERS

During the course of a normal week, analyze a situation in your interaction with somebody (at work, family, or socially) that demonstrated your high-level Hypersensitive Thinking.

Ask Yourself:

What situations are causing me to be Hypersensitive and take things personally? What circumstances triggered me to misinterpret what people were saying?

What would I like to change if I was to have another chance at the previous situation? How did I let my emotions overrule sound judgment?

How is this counterproductive communication with people?

Does being Hypersensitive make me feel embarrassed around others?

How is Hypersensitive Thinking impacting my relationships with people, family, coworkers, and friends?

> *"Folly is joy to him who is destitute of discernment, But a man of understanding walks uprightly."*
>
> Proverbs 15:21 (nkjv)

Most people are Hypersensitive on at least some level, and this fearful thinking holds most people back in some form from being themselves. This is all the more reason to understand Christ wants us to not be Hypersensitive. So, let's not take things personally and instead be more Christ-like in how we interact with others.

In Scripture we are told "do not be afraid." We are not made to take on others' problems personally. Jesus was extremely confident and was always in an observation mode and kept things that people said and did neutral. He simply watched their behavior but didn't take on their issues. Nor should you because you are made in God's image.

Story of Jessica

Jessica just started her new job as a bank teller. She was so excited because this was the best bank in town. Her coworkers were friendly, warm, and outgoing. They frequently went to lunch together and had a great time.

This bank did a lot of commercial business, so there were many local business owners who came to her window. As in all businesses, there were some very demanding business customers, and you guessed it—they would come to Jessica's window. Several of these customers were critical, disagreeable, and argumentative. When customers like this left her window, Jessica often felt down, offended, angry, and hurt. She took the critical customer's problems personally, so much so that she was considering quitting her job. Her productivity at work began to falter, and she would feel so depressed she started calling in sick to work. This developed a pattern the teller manager noticed.

Upon her quarterly review, she was put on probation for poor attendance. Jessica complained to the manager about the critical customers. The manager kept focusing on Jessica's poor attendance. This infuriated Jessica to the point of filing a stress claim. How could this problem have been solved? What if Jessica was not controlled by her Hypersensitive Thinking? How could the manager have helped Jessica with this?

Jesus is very objective and is NOT Hypersensitive. This is why the Pharisees could not get to Him. You are built in the image of God. You are built to be very objective and view people and their actions like Jesus did. You can do this!

EXAMINING THE IMPACT

High levels of Hypersensitive Thinking are among the biggest stresses in our businesses today. We see it in many situations. For example, a Hypersensitive person may walk into an office and get an anxiety rush when everyone stares at him. Everyone stares because he's a new arrival, but the Hypersensitive person embarrassingly thinks, "What's wrong with me? Why are people looking at me?" Similarly, a new employee will be uneasy about her performance on her first day. She may become anxious at the simplest of questions. She may misinterpret what other people say and inevitably experience hurt feelings. She overpersonalizes other coworkers' looks, tones of voice, and even silence—interpreting these as negative. These overreactions may seem very inappropriate to other people and, when confronted, the Hypersensitive person may even get defensive. For no apparent reason, a high Hypersensitive person may blurt out a remark that is "off base or very embarrassing." The emotions overrule the judgment and a struggle develops between reality and what the Hypersensitive person perceives as reality. But it's an inaccurate reality.

Have you experienced this type of thinking in a coworker or family member? What happened? Can you imagine a work environment where no one got his or her feelings hurt or overreacted; a place where you didn't have to tip toe around worrying about offending someone when your intentions are good?

> *"Jesus said to him, 'I am the way, the truth, and the life. No one comes to the Father except through Me. If you had known Me, you would have known My Father also; and from now on you know Him and have seen Him.'"*
>
> JOHN 14:6-7 (NKJV)

By being able to recognize and understand the behaviors of those with high Hypersensitive Thinking levels you will be better able to help them in increasing their confidence and improving their communication.

How do you observe this Hypersensitive Thinking in yourself or others?

In what situations have you been involved with an individual with a high level of Hypersensitive Thinking?

What barriers to communication do you see as being a result of having a high level of Hypersensitive Thinking?

In what ways can these behaviors be turned around to improve communication?

YOUR PERSONAL DEVELOPMENT PLAN

Up to this point, you have spent some time gaining a deeper understanding of Hypersensitive Thinking and examining the impact of personal behaviors in relationships and in your world of work. Now you are ready to begin the process of building increased confidence and reducing Hypersensitive Thinking.

Simple Exercises to Stop Feeling Hypersensitive

We can change our thinking and understand that each exercise is a learning process. There are no failing steps in life's journey. There is only failure if we stop moving forward. So, we must prove to ourselves that we can learn beyond the first obstacle. Accept yourself for being human. No human can do everything right! Mistakes or perceived failures are "opportunities" to learn and grow.

As you apply each of the following exercises, monitor your progress by noting down situations that occur during the coming weeks, in which you applied each exercise.

Recognize That the World Does Not Center Around You

This doesn't mean you are not important. You are important. What it means is that the world and the people in it are not out to get you and hurt you. They are absorbed in their own problems and concerns. In fact, if you look outward, away from yourself, you'll discover that other people are probably more Hypersensitive than you. So, take the pressure off yourself. You aren't in the spotlight. Practice focusing outward and "observing others' issues" to get your mind off your worries—do this two times per day.

Keep It Neutral

Learn not to read a tone of voice, or a glance, as negative. Turn off your Hypersensitive emotions and stay objective. When someone looks at you, he may be just as worried about your opinions of him. If someone does try to stare you down in a negative way, then he owns the problem, so don't buy into his problem. Practice keeping things neutral three times this week.

Listen to the Content of What Someone Says

Again, keep it neutral. For example, your boss says in a gruff voice, "When are you going to get the job done?" Now, listen to the content. He's not saying you are a poor performer. He is just asking about the completion date. He may be having a bad day. It could be that his abrupt tone has nothing to do with you. Make your day a good one by keeping everything neutral and concentrating on the content of what people say.

Allow Your Intellect to Overrule Your Negative Emotions

When you feel an emotional reaction—sweaty palms, flushed face—take a deep breath. Slow down. Concentrate on sound judgment. Decide not to react before thinking the situation through. Then respond in a positive manner. When in doubt, check it out. Reality is only as clear as we choose to understand it. Do this daily this week.

Choose Reality, Rather Than Just Perceived Reality

Perceived reality is when we are thinking a little "off base." It is outside of reality. It is attaching hurt feelings and/or unnecessary negative feelings to a neutral reality (what others are really saying or meaning). For example: A friend is staring out into space and just happens to glance in your direction with a blank, far-off look. You may feel she is reacting negatively toward you. "Is something wrong with my appearance? Make-up? Hair uncombed?" That may only be your perception, or your perceived reality. Reality is that your friend is deep in thought. If you waved your hands in front of her eyes you would probably discover that she isn't thinking about you at all. She may be thinking of work or tomorrow's weekend adventure. To overcome your sensitivity issue, you must end the negative perceptions and stay in objective reality.

Don't Let Anyone Wreck Your Day

Recognize that nobody can wreck your day without you giving that person permission. The only way you can own somebody else's problem is if you "buy into it." It's like a car salesman trying to sell you a car you don't want. You can listen to him, but you don't need to buy the car. You can walk away and still feel okay about yourself. For Example: Let's imagine you are having a picnic on a Sunday afternoon in your back yard. You're barbecuing chicken. You have friends over and family. On the other side of the fence, you have a neighbor – they are also barbecuing chicken. But there are flames coming out of their chicken, you hear them swearing, you see smoke coming, and bellowing out – they are not having a good day! Can you imagine inviting your neighbor over, and having them burn your chicken?! Don't let anybody spoil your day! Keep a lot of things neutral! - Don't let anyone burn your chicken!

> *"Though an army may encamp against me, my heart shall not fear; Though war may rise against me, In this I will be confident."*
>
> Psalms 27:3 (NKJV)

Hypersensitive Thinking–Transformational Thinking Statements

Truths to Set Your Thinking Free

Check all that apply to you:

_____I am built in the image of God. I will be very objective and view people and their actions, keeping it neutral just like Jesus did.

_____I choose to keep looks that people give me, and their tone of voice, neutral.

_____Around 95 percent of what people say is neutral—so I won't take other peoples' words, looks, or silences personally. I will be objective like Christ.

_____Most of what others say and do is neutral; therefore, I will not read into their actions.

_____If someone is REALLY NEGATIVE, I will recognize that he or she owns the problem.

_____Nobody is going to burn my chicken—it is their issue if they are really negative.

_____I choose not to buy into other people's problems. I will stay neutral.

_____I'm keeping "looks," "people's tones of voice," and "silence" neutral.

_____I'm not responsible for someone else's problem unless I deliberately try to cause that person a problem.

_____I choose to listen to the **content** of what others say and keep it neutral.

_____I choose to have a great day. Nobody is going to wreck my day. I will have a Christ-like attitude when around others.

_____I choose to focus outward and not overpersonalize situations.

_____I will be in an observation mode; I will watch other people's issues but not buy into their problems. Christ didn't buy in to the Pharisees' problems.

_____I will be in an observation mode without thinking negative thoughts. I will just watch the show when others are out of control.

_____When I am in doubt, I should check it out. I will ask and not assume I know what others are thinking. I will get it verified before I jump to negative conclusions.

_____I choose to take charge of my fears through Christ and not let the fears take charge of me.

_____People want to hear my ideas, so I will speak up with Christ-like thinking and actions.

Read your Transformational Thinking Statements three to five times a day or as needed.

> "Oh, how great is Your goodness, Which You have laid up for those who fear You, Which You have prepared for those who trust in You In the presence of the sons of men!"
>
> PSALMS 31:19 (NKJV)

> "... be transformed by the renewing of your mind...."
>
> ROMANS 12:2 (NKJV)

"For God so loved the world that He gave His only begotten Son, that whoever believes in Him should not perish but have everlasting life."

JOHN 3:16 (NKJV)

NOTES

CHAPTER 12

SPIRITUAL SURVIVAL

Answers to a Life-Changing Subject?

Spiritual Survival Is the Foundation for Your Life and Existence

Although this chapter is saved for last, it is the most important of all chapters of this book. Why put it for last? Because it is the foundation of real change in a person's life. Your soul is the foundation for your building, which keeps your life a purposeful, living structure.

If you have a poor foundation in a building, the building will shift, teeter, or completely fail and fall until you provide a stronger foundation to make it stronger. If there is no foundation, then the building will crumble from the elements of time, wind, weather, and so on. Likewise, a person that doesn't have a spiritual foundation (Spiritual Survival) will always be searching for "something to fill the eternal void inside." This eternal void has only one solution that fills this void.

Philosophies don't fill this void, chants don't fill this void, metaphysical ideologies don't fill this void, religious doxologies don't fill this void, rituals don't fill this void, worshiping idols doesn't fill this void, and so on. So, what does fill our inner void that yearns to be fulfilled? It all goes back to Spiritual Survival. Why are you here on earth? What is your purpose? Why are you made in God's image?

Spiritual Survival is the highest form of survival and relationships we can have as humans. People can't survive without a spirit. When your spirit leaves your body, they call it being dead, but one's soul lives on. But where does it go?

In the beginning of this book we talked about one's Primary Relationship as a key element of Spiritual Survival. Spiritual Survival is the highest form of survival, and these are the key elements.

The most important element is your relationship with God, who describes Himself as the Great I AM, God the Father, Jesus the Son, and the Holy Spirit. Talk to a person that has committed his or her life to a relationship with the Lord and you'll notice something very different with that person. He or she has an inner peace, joy, and a fulfilled heart. This is a real relationship that fills an inner vacancy (void that only Christ can fill). This provides a purpose to our existence and helps people to be able to answer the question "Who am I?" without reservation because they know they are a child of God. This creates an inner spiritual fulfillment when a person "knows their sins are forgiven." This lifts the person's inner being, the human spirit, because he or she knows that these represent a "free ticket to heaven." Note that "it's not about being good to gain heaven," it's about being forgiven.

"How can we be so sure?" you may ask. Because these individuals have a Primary Relationship with the One who loves them so much. Jesus died on a cross to save them and this includes you as well. This is a felt compassion with the One who created us and loves us.

This is not just an ideology, or a metaphysical philosophy, or a religion. No!

It's a real, loving, heart-filled relationship with a Creator, a real Person, a Friend that cares for you in real life, now.

This is a communicated love, not a dogmatic religion.

It's coming to the realization that Jesus died for your sins, with no strings attached. It's you coming to Him to accept this gift of forgiveness. Oh, and no, you can't be perfect before your friend accepts you, or forgives you. It's all about receiving a gift even when you don't deserve it. It's receiving forgiveness and being genuinely grateful for the gift of forgiveness. No more guilt! All you have to do is say "thank you" and accept the gift. It's that easy, and it works if you open your heart to being forgiven and sincerely wanting a real relationship with a loving God (this is what fills the void with your Lord and Savior).

This brings about another part of Spiritual Survival, and that is communication with the Lord on a Primary Relationship basis, expressing your love and thankfulness (worship for his compassion and caring for you). This also includes communicating on a feeling level or emotional relating, which is an important part of primary relating. Yes, you can have a Primary Relationship (real friendship with the Lord), and you will never be alone again.

Having a real relationship with the Lord is the strongest foundation for your life. It is the best decision you will ever make, it is the deepest relationship you can have, and it never runs out, because above all you know that you will spend eternity in heaven even if you are not perfect, which is why Jesus had to die for your sins and mine.

I can tell you my life was empty beyond empty until I let Jesus in and realized I was forgiven. I had to teach myself to believe this statement: "God accepts me as a human being with faults." I wrote this on a piece of paper and carried it around with me for a very long time, until it was written in my heart. I have known hundreds of people that have this realization, and began a life journey choosing a Primary Relationship with the Lord, and they all have one thing in common: They are forgiven and they have joy; they don't feel alone, and have a reassuring peace because they have the assurance of everlasting life.

And here is what a few of them have said about how their lives have changed:

= = =

Before I made the choice to accept the Lord into my life, I put much effort into making things happen—doing to achieve. "If it was to be it was up to me!" was a strong philosophy of mine. I achieved much but without the cord of three (Ecc. 4:12) that strengthens lives and relationships.

I had the opportunity to get into God's Word through the people He put around me, after going through a divorce that I was not prepared for. I came to understand through His Word that man's ways were not His ways, that I was free to marry again and fulfill His desire for my life.

Once again, He had a plan that was different from my expectation. My spouse was diagnosed and died of cancer within a year; rather than a long and happy life together, we had a short, intense, intimate, caring, and precious journey. Again, I was blessed to be supported by the Spirit in knowing God had blessed me with the privilege of being able to be with and look after this cherished soul giving him five wonderful years at the end of his short life.

Then God had another plan for my life. For the last ten years I have been working in a field helping people through their changes, losses, and trials, and providing opportunities for couples and individuals to get to know the power of the Lord in their lives and relationships. For a couple, prayer together is one of the most intimate and connecting things a couple can do, creating transparency, connection, intimacy, and joint purpose and direction as well as a reliance on a power greater than themselves to resolve trials as they develop. When I accepted the Almighty into my life I was filled with an acceptance, for there is no more regret or frustration, or wondering and hoping for something different.

I now possess a calming acceptance that I am in God's hands, my life is His to direct and influence; that He has a plan greater than any I could come up with since He has known me before I was born. He has known the trials I would be exposed to and would bring me through them, with truth, love, and a lamp unto my feet in times of darkness.

This knowledge and peace that passes all understanding has changed my life forever, with a calm understanding that no matter what happens, He is there to guide me and I am His child, treasured and loved by Him, our God Almighty.

- Annie V.

===

I was a young scientist whose life was completely self-centered and where only physical reality was important. I was an alcoholic with a marriage nearing divorce. One Saturday, on my birthday, my wife had an accident and broke her back. She was paralyzed, the medical specialist said, "for the rest of her life." My life was shattered. No medical insurance, two very young kids, and a wife who would need me to take care of her for the rest of her life. And we had moved to a new town where I knew no one who could help. I was alone and at the lowest point of my life. But . . . five days later my wife got out of her hospital bed and walked to the chapel to thank her God for miraculously healing her. Somehow our life had been restored to us. Her doctor called it "a miracle."

I spent the next year reading the Bible and seeking to know if there was a reality beyond the physical and empty one I knew. One day while reading the Bible I stopped and said, "Lord, if all of this I'm reading is true, I want to really understand it and follow You." It was as if a shade had been lifted in front of my eyes. The Bible became alive and I could connect the various parts. They meshed together and painted this beautiful picture of a loving, forgiving, understanding, and patient God who had come to earth and died for me so that I could know Him personally forever. Wow! Talk about reality setting in! My life became exciting, fresh, and full. This LORD whom I now knew as Jesus, God's Son, healed me in many ways over these last 37 years . . . my marriage, alcoholism, self-centeredness, inability to love, no direction for my life. And He has given me a full life while preparing me for the one that is to follow this one.

I started out my adult life wanting, as Albert Einstein did, to know the Mind of God and instead was born anew to desire and know the Heart of God. It is wonderful to have a personal relationship with the Living God. There is a Reality far beyond the physical one we see with our natural eyes . . . seek Him, desire Him, and accept Him. There is nothing better to be found in the universe!

- Bob W.

= = =

I was raised as a Reform Jew in Los Angeles. I never really related to religion, nor did I ever believe in the actual existence of God. Thus, of course, I stopped going to Temple as soon as I could, at 16. Before being saved, and accepting Jesus in 2008, at 63 years of age, I had led what most would consider a fairly decent life. However, it was filled with the kind of excess and hedonism that I now believe is sinful.

I had two failed marriages. I never believed in any higher power, and I had no real "life goals." I was kind to most people, but not at all spiritual. I got married a third time in 1997. In 2005, due to some surprise circumstances, my wife Angelia and I adopted a 2-year-old little girl—Sydney. We decided that we did not want to raise her in California, and, for some unknown reason, we wanted to raise her with a religious foundation. So, we chose my wife's childhood faith—Christian/Baptist.

In 2006 a job opportunity presented itself and we moved from Santa Barbara to Dallas and found a sweet community church. We attended as a family, and I began to learn the basics. I also began to see my journey, tracing back to the start of my marriage to Angelia. A thread ran through our marriage, adopting Sydney, moving to Dallas, and ultimately being born again. It is cliché to say that my life had no meaningful center before, but that is the truth. I was fine and in fact mostly happy, but my core was pretty much mush. I had no absolute spiritual beliefs or values.

After attending our new church in Plano, Texas, for a year I discovered what I consider to be proof of the existence of God.* The realization, and the recognition of His ultimate and awesome power, then led me to the acceptance of the Lord Jesus Christ as my Savior, and the Holy Trinity.

It was divine intervention that we landed in this particular place and discovered a pastor who preached the simplicity of the Bible as truth; God; and an intimate personal relationship with His Son Jesus Christ. In 2008 we traveled with our Bible study class to the Holy Land. During this trip, I was baptized in the River Jordan with Sydney (my daughter, then age 5). Since that time there has not been one day that I have not prayed and thanked the Lord for bringing me to this point. I have had some very difficult times financially since early 2008, but for reasons that I still cannot explain my faith has remained solid, as I wait, watch, and listen to what God has in store for me and my family, as my story unwinds toward an end—slowly, I hope.

I know now what the final chapter in my life will be. I am confident that I will spend eternity with my Lord, my wife, Sydney, and a lot of friends. I have hope for our other children, but no guarantees. I live every day with excitement about what God might do with me, constantly asking for His guidance. He has blessed us by surrounding us with a multitude of fellow believers who continue to share our faith and enrich our lives in Christ. Anyone who ever knew me before 2008 could read this 1,000 times and still not believe that I wrote it.

*My personal proof of the existence of God:

- The Bible states that long before man existed the earth was once covered with water.
- Science now universally confirms this.
- The first five books of the Old Testament (known as the Pentateuch or Torah) are thought to be written by Moses during the forty years that the children of Israel wandered in the wilderness (1450–1410 B.C). It is also possible that the information contained in these first five books had been passed down from Babylonian and Canaanite myths and legends and from Israel's own "legends" and "oral tradition." One theory is that it might have originally come from Abraham, Jacob, Noah, and even Adam. None of these theories argue that any of these sources (men) were present on earth at the time it was actually covered with water.
- Therefore, if there was in fact no man on earth at the time it was covered with water, who told the first person the true story?

I believe that the only logical answer proves the existence of God.

--- Dennis

CONCLUSION

YOUR NEW BEGINNING

Some Thoughtful Encouragement

A lot of people think that they have to earn their way to heaven. The truth is there is nothing you can do to "earn your way to heaven." A ticket to heaven is not for sale. It's a free gift from God. All you have to do is want it with all your heart and ask for forgiveness. Why ask for forgiveness? Because if you have hurt someone and you want to make amends you ask for forgiveness, so you reestablish the relationship. Then you tell your friend that you want him or her back in your life.

Do you have any idea how important you are to your Creator? Your Creator wants a relationship with you, but He is polite and is waiting for you to ask Him into your life. Like those you just read about, I hope you find this very encouraging to hear how God changes lives, and how God fills that vacant hole that only He can fill in your heart and life. I encourage you to read the Bible every day. It may take you three years to complete it; that's no problem. It will be the best book you will ever read because it is God's Word.

As you have asked God into your life, I encourage you to also take time to read the insightful chapters, examples, and foundational tools found in this book to help you "to be transformed by the renewing of your mind" and equip you to fully develop your life, so you may better understand yourself and others.

Our Pride Can Be Very Costly

We can be stubborn and only want life to be the way we want it and think we don't need God, or any other relationships, for us to get what we want out of life. Ask people with more experience in life, and they can tell you they have made lots of mistakes, and give you horror stories of how their stubbornness and pride has ruined their lives: Lost relationships, fears, drugs, accidents, depression, anger, and lack of direction and purpose. Your life doesn't need to fall in a life of lonely desperation.

You Are Here for a Reason!

You are so important that God created you in HIS image. You were made for a higher purpose. There is a hole in every person's heart that can only be filled by the One who made you. He wants a personal relationship with you, so much so, he sent Jesus, who died for all your sins. **Now that is Love in Action.** This—God's love—is the missing piece in every person's heart.

We Can't Earn Salvation, It's a Gift.

All you have to do is be thankful for this gift and have faith in Jesus, God's Son, and ask for forgiveness and invite Him into your heart. This establishes your relationship with HIM. So, we turn from our sins, which is called repentance or transforming our thinking to following Christ. Jesus knows you and loves you, and what matters to Him is your Heart to have an honest relationship with Him.

The Gift of Everlasting Life

Jesus is polite. We are given free will to choose a relationship of joy and having everlasting life with Him in heaven if we ask. Not a bad deal - Just asking for forgiveness and wanting a relationship with Jesus and His Father God for eternal life. Wow! It's that simple.

> "... *choose for yourselves this day whom you will serve.* ..."
>
> Joshua 24:15 (NKJV)

If you choose to receive the gift of everlasting life, and Christ in your heart, it is as simple as praying this prayer from your heart and your spirit:

"Dear Lord God,

I know I'm a sinner, and I ask for your loving forgiveness.

I believe Jesus is God's Son who died for all my sins.

You raised Jesus from the dead,

Jesus, I ask the Holy Spirit into my life. Be my Lord and Savior. I will follow you Lord, from this day forward.

Guide my life and help me to do your will.

Thank you, Father God, for forgiving me, saving me, and giving me eternal life.

I pray this in the name of Jesus. Amen."

> *"For whoever calls on the name of the LORD shall be saved."*
>
> ROMANS 10:13 (NKJV)

> *"For God so loved the world that He gave His only begotten Son, that whoever believes in Him should not perish but have everlasting life."*
>
> JOHN 3:16 (NKJV)

If you honestly, with your heart, prayed this prayer and really meant it— Welcome to a new transformed life in Christ! This is the best decision in life you can ever make . . . because you are made in God's image.

All blessings to you!
Gary Morais

About the Author

This book is written because of a driving need to help God's people, by equipping them to reach their fullness in how they were created and to discover their God-given inner gifts and hidden strengths so they can better understand how they have been built in "the image of Christ."

I say this because I came to realize that in my own life and the lives of thousands of people I have worked with over the last thirty-five years, we are wonderfully made, by a Creator that loves us. I didn't always understand this, because my own personal journey in life didn't start out so wonderfully. But that's life!

My personal life journey started out a little rocky with me dying at birth. Had it not been for a good old country doctor and his determination to revive me, this book would never have been written. Yes, God is good, and He saves in so many ways!

I grew up amid a very painful home life. My father was a good man, but very confused; he was abused by his father and as a result of his lack of life skills became a raging alcoholic. My mother was left on her own at around age 13 when her mother died, and her father just lost it and crumbled because of the loss of his wife. The best way to describe my family life from around 12 to 18 years old was "living in a war zone." This led me to be a lost individual that was always trying to please everybody and not have a life of my own, which brought me to a level of deep depression. Yes, life can deal us some difficult challenges, but if you let those stop you then you will never find the inner joy and love that awaits you through a loving Savior in whose image you are made in.

It was hard for my parents to provide me with life skills when they had few tools of their own, but some things that I did get from my parents were how to work hard, be as good as your word, and love people, as well as receiving real encouragement from my mother.

In 1968, Viet Nam was in full swing. I was working my way through college because my family could not afford to pay for it. I ended up having surgery for a bone tumor. As a result of the surgery, I ended up with a blood clot in my lower right leg, which caused the calf of my leg to swell to a much larger than normal size and remain that way for about 8 years. Looking back, God's grace was at work, because it kept me from being shipped to Viet Nam, but it didn't keep me from my depression. My life was in shambles, with little money and no direction. A good way to describe it was I was just existing in the sea of life, bobbing around like a cork, being shifted by the waves of life and feeling totally lost, and on the brink of suicidal thoughts. I tell you this not to gain sympathy, but to illustrate there is always hope even when you least expect it, and for me hope was just about to take place. Prayer kept me alive.

My desperation was quite great when I heard of a retreat that was to take place in Three Rivers, California. I learned about it when I was attending the Newman Center (this is where the college kids went to church). Something told me I had to do something for myself, because I was so depleted, depressed, lost, and empty. So, I picked up two other college kids in my bright yellow VW bus, and we set out for the mountains.

My depression was pervasive; it stemmed from things I did in my early childhood that I was embarrassed and felt very guilty about. Now others may say these were normal things all kids go through, but for me they were deep burdens. I felt like this sin was unforgivable, and that I needed to make up for my sin by being a "goody two shoes" to gain God's favor. This was an unending cycle of pain and suffering in my mind. I can truly tell you that sin is not a pleasant experience and my pain was all encompassing. Well, my life was about to change in the blink of an eye.

We had a time in the retreat when we could go and have a private time with the retreat master, who happened to be 4 feet 11 inches tall with a loving heart much bigger than his body. This is where I spilled my heart out in repentance, looking for peace and acceptance, and found that God forgave all my sins and loved me, a human being with faults. Here is where I met the real Jesus personally, and allowed Him into my life, because I finally realized that I had a loving, forgiving Father who cared about me and wanted what was best for me. My life changed forever, in the blink of an eye, thanks to the Savior of the world. The burden of sin was lifted, and I was transformed into a Spirit-filled human being. Wow!

I realized we are all fallible, and that this is why Jesus died on the cross to set us free from our sins. Boy, what a relief. My depression lifted instantaneously, in the blink of an eye. A giant burden came off of me and I can tell you that was the day my life changed, and I started to really live. I went up the mountain lonely, lost, and depressed and came down the mountain a new person in Christ with a fresh start free from the burdens of sin that I had felt. What a breath of fresh air from a forgiving, loving God.

Although this was a huge transition, I still struggled because my family didn't equip me with how to deal with daily life issues like confidence, people skills, career, relationships, parenthood, problem solving, and leadership, just for starters. I didn't even know what happiness was. I thought it was some secret other people knew about, and I didn't know how to even know how to find it. I was plagued by Self-Doubt, Self-Defeating Thoughts; I was Hypersensitive and took most things personally; was still looking for self-assurance from others, and was very poor at making a decision on my own. Yes, this was my "bobbing cork" wimp-in-the-sea-of-life-syndrome. Yet I knew God loved me, so why did I have this gnawing frustration and anxiety that made my joints hurt? I didn't know the secret of "how to understand myself and others." That was to come later.

Well, I graduated, and because of my work as a college student at the Newman Center, I was offered a job as director of youth ministry, and this is where I discovered that my passion in life was people. I got married and soon after my wife became pregnant with our first child. But I was still a wimp and still struggled with Self-Doubting, Self-Defeating Thoughts, I was still Hypersensitive and took most things personally, I was still looking for self-assurance from others.

I was determined that I did not want to pass this on to my child like my parents did with me. I was determined to "refine myself," to "transform myself" into the person God made me to be, even if I didn't know what it was, I had to make it happen for my child. The reason I tell you this is because this was another turning point to step out in faith even if I didn't know the results, in order to be the person God was calling me to be. Well it took me three years of intense counseling and learning, being equipped by two Christian counselors, to whom I am forever grateful. In Romans 12:2 it says "be transformed by the renewing of your mind" (NJKV). Yes, we all can be transformed, and this book is designed to help you to be transformed by renewing your mind and life.

This book is written to equip you with life skills and tools learned from thirty-five years of bite size solutions that have helped thousands of people from all walks of life, to give you the secrets of what makes people tick. This book is meant to provide you with knowledge that has helped people change their lives by renewing their minds and trading up to the Biblical wisdom and thinking Scripture talks about. May I add just one thing? The best psychological book I have ever read is the Bible! For some of you, this may come as a surprise. I know it was for me, also.

So, ask yourself this: "Do I have eyes to see? Do I have ears to hear? Do I have a heart to want to know and gain real wisdom?" Reading this book to equip yourself may take some courage, with the willingness to grow, to have eyes that want to see life differently, ears that want to hear, and a heart that wants to grow and "be transformed by the renewing of your mind." This is my wish: hope, encouragement, and prayer for you, to come to the complete fullness of Christ in your heart, mind, and soul that you may have a more fulfilled life, and to become more Christ-like because you are mightily made in His image.

All of God's blessings to you!
Gary Morais

Printed in the USA
CPSIA information can be obtained
at www.ICGtesting.com
JSHW012015081223
53468JS00001B/1